That (

That Other Voice

In search of a God who speaks

To my dear and much-respected friend Robin

Graham Turner

Graham September 2017

DARTON · LONGMAN + TODD

First published in Great Britain in 2017 by
Darton, Longman and Todd Ltd
1 Spencer Court
140–142 Wandsworth High Street
London SW18 4JJ

ISBN 978-0-232-53327-9

A catalogue record for this book is available from the British Library.

The poem 'Ordinary God' by Donald Davie is reproduced by kind
permission of Carcanet Press Limited.

Typeset by Kerrypress Ltd, St Albans

Printed and bound by Bell & Bain, Glasgow

'Hope' is the thing with feathers -
That perches in the soul -
And sings the tune without the words -
And never stops - at all -

And sweetest - in the Gale - is heard -
And sore must be the storm -
That could abash the little Bird
That kept so many warm -

I've heard it in the chillest land -
And on the strangest Sea -
Yet - never - in Extremity,
It asked a crumb - of me.

Hope **by Emily Dickinson**

Contents

Foreword

Perhaps the most urgent question anyone ever asks is, 'Can real change be possible?' – change in the power relations in the world, in the level of suffering and frustration that so many people live with daily, change (above all) in myself, with all my mechanisms of defence and fear and acquisitiveness. To answer this question simply in terms of conventional religious or moral teaching won't really do: there are plenty of people making the right noises, but not many of those noises are truly heard and understood: plenty of teaching, you might say, but not much learning.

Graham Turner, in this vivid and sensitive book, introduces us to a wide variety of people who have actually learned about change by learning to listen at a new level of intensity. The voice of God comes in many forms, and we see just how diversely it can be heard in people's complex human experience. What emerges most steadily in these stories is the difference that is made by two simple – but immensely demanding – things: honesty and patience. We need to risk laying bare some of what we are most eager to hide from others and from ourselves, to bring things out into the daylight so that we can understand and deal with them – habits of mind and behaviour, memories and ambitions and traumas. And we need to take time to allow the truth we seek to sink in and to transform us.

This is the very opposite of a naive belief that there is an inner light that will give us infallible guidance in our problems. On the contrary it is about developing habits of silence and attention, scrutinising without self-indulgence the byways of our 'inner life', and nurturing a basic trust that truth exists and will change us and our world if only we allow it space enough. Graham Turner has written a hopeful but very challenging book about how those he writes about have learned this sort of vision and discipline, and he offers a timely, realistic orientation towards a renewal of the spirit in our culture.

ROWAN WILLIAMS
Master of Magdalene College, Cambridge
Formerly Archbishop of Canterbury (2002-2012)

Preface

This book is the product of a journey – a journey that took me to many parts of India and to Jordan, as well as all over Britain. It was a journey that led to conversations with Muslims, Hindus, Buddhists and Jews as well as Christians, and it contained its own minor moments of peril.

It was a journey in search of an answer to the ultimate spiritual mystery – whether God or a higher power of some kind, can communicate with us directly in what we might call that other 'voice'. By 'voice' I don't for the most part mean words that seem to be spoken out loud so much as clear and commanding thoughts which seem to come from elsewhere, and down a different channel from that of our own minds. Conscience too, speaks to virtually all of us in a silent but nonetheless potent way.

The devout, of most faiths, (though not Buddhists), would respond that, of course, there is a God and that he communicates best with us through holy texts of various kinds; and that the inspiration of those texts has led them into the glory of new lives.

A good many other people, by contrast, would answer that their conception of the divine power speaks to them most clearly through the glories of nature or through music that stirs them deeply. Others again would say that some kind of divine power had made its presence felt during crises of one sort or another or even, sometimes, through the words of candid friends.

God, if God it be, does seem to be rather unscrupulous: He will use any number of ways to get through to us.

I wouldn't for a moment deny any of these experiences, but I wanted to ask whether that divine power can communicate with all or any of us, in one way or another, as God spoke to the prophets of old. Okay, very few of us are prophets of any kind, but we are still said by the devout to be made in the image of God, and so the question is still valid.

I also began the journey because I have had experiences of my own which predispose me to believe that there is a guiding spirit at work in the universe, and I wanted to find out not only whether people of other faiths (I am a Christian) have had similar experiences, but also what the outcome in their lives has been. After all, if God does not act in the world, people might reasonably ask, what is the point of Him?

A number of the stories I tell here are of people known to me and trusted by me, who come from a religious background similar to my own. So an organisation called Initiatives of Change (formally Moral Rearmament) will keep popping up throughout the book. I am not a propagandist for IofC - which is now very modest in size and influence – but I value the religious experiences of those I write about. Many are rather unusual stories but I imagine that people who come from traditions similar to my own could produce similar ones.

I am conscious that I have offered, perhaps, too little in the way of theological comment and analysis on these stories.

By way of excuse, I have borne in mind that the Christian Gospels are, in large part, a collection of stories, anecdotes and incidents that offer little in the way of theological analysis. I hope that the stories in this book will, in their depth and simplicity, make their own point.

One

That Other Voice

That other voice? What other voice are you talking about, you may well ask? It's a perfectly fair question, because I'm not talking about the voice produced by our vocal chords, from the merest of whispers to the torrent of sound which poured forth from a singer such as Pavarotti. (Pavarotti, incidentally, occasionally registered 94 decibels. 194 decibels is the loudest sound recorded.)

No, what I'm talking about is the third definition offered by the Oxford English Dictionary – 'the supposed utterance of a guiding spirit'.

On the face of things, that sounds rather airy-fairy. After all, since such a 'voice' is only 'heard' within a person, what kind of substance or objective reality can it possibly have? Whatever its hearers may claim, it can never be *proven* to have taken place at all.

Hence, no doubt, the fact that, in the dictionary definition, it is merely 'supposed' to have happened and that its content is given no more precise attribution than the somewhat dismissive 'utterance'.

And what are we supposed to infer from the words 'guiding spirit'? Are we talking about God or some other kind of inspirational force? Anyone who claims to have heard from the Almighty is widely thought to be not merely credulous but in urgent need of psychiatric help. That would certainly once have been thought to apply to anyone who said they had heard 'voices' in the plural.

In any event, might not whatever people claim to have heard be merely the gymnastics of our remarkable brains, a projection of our super-ego, a psychological phenomenon and nothing more?

The whole idea of a guiding spirit, what is more, does seem to presuppose the existence of an essentially benevolent deity – though how anyone can have the effrontery blithely to maintain that there is such a god at work in the world without somehow accounting for events such as the Holocaust, the continuing horrors in countries such as Syria and the apparently random operation of good or bad fortune – I cannot imagine.

Even the shrewdest of religious professionals is wary of promoting any such bland assumption. 'The world is full of tragedies and disasters,' said Christopher Lewis, the former Dean of Christ Church, Oxford, 'not to mention the grinding misery of ordinary life for so many'.

People were bound to ask why God had chosen to exclude them from the blessings that the devout claimed to have received. 'Why not me and why not now?', they might respond. 'No,' they'd say, 'so far as we're concerned, life is a bitch and then you die!'

His own rule of thumb in these matters, the Dean went on, was that nothing should ever be attributed to God unless it could not easily be explained in any other way, unless it simply cried out for other than a rational explanation.

And yet, and yet … people who appear to be perfectly sane claim to have had experiences of God guiding them, or of having had religious experiences which have transformed their lives. Nor are revelatory experiences that seem to descend out of the blue confined to Christians. Zen Buddhists speak of *sartori*, a Japanese word for awakening, which shows itself in the sudden flashing into consciousness of insights hitherto undreamt of.

Sufi Muslims – who come from a mystical tradition and describe Sufism as 'the beating heart of Islam' – talk about *waridat*, spiritual experiences which also come upon them suddenly out of the blue. As one English Sufi put it: 'They take over your whole soul and you feel absolutely certain that they are from God. They definitely aren't self-generated psychological happenings that you've been pushing for'. Often, he added, a *warid* came as an intuition about the road you should take in life.

In his own experience, they arrived with a force that demanded to be obeyed. 'One day', he recalled, 'I received a *warid* which pointed out something in my own life which wasn't actually sinful but wasn't spiritually optimal either. I felt I must get rid of it, though strictly I didn't need to. That *warid* hit me in the heart, I knew it was from God. It was a piece of direction which changed my life.'

For ardent Hindus, too, all great spiritual truths lie within us and are revealed to those open to receive them. 'Every human being', said Dr Amit Mukherjee, an orthopaedic surgeon from Jamshedpur, 'is *sat-chit-ananda* – truth,

3

wisdom, bliss – which means that all truth, wisdom and happiness lie within.'

He went on: 'That other voice of which you speak lies waiting to speak to us every moment of our lives. I've never myself heard it as a voice. I call it 'sparks', sudden inspirations which are completely different from our normal thought processes. Those "sparks" come from within.'

On the other hand, the vast majority of Jews, according to a leading liberal rabbi, Jonathan Romain, have no time for the notion of a God who speaks to them or for such divinely-inspired 'sparks'; and Tibetan Buddhists, who do not believe in a god at all, have a very different approach to the idea of inspiration from above. For them, the idea of a guiding spirit is much more acceptable.

According to those who claim to have received these 'sparks', these intimations of the divine, they come in a variety of guises. Occasionally, they arrive with what Christian monks and nuns call 'interior locutions'. In other words, they have the quality of an actual voice speaking within, a voice so clear that the hearer will sometimes look round to see who has spoken and so authoritatively that they demand to be obeyed.

There is a good fictional example of an interior locution in C. J. Sansom's Tudor thriller *Dissolution*. The hunchback lawyer, Matthew Shardlake, Sansom's detective, recalls how he was insulted as a young man when he told a monk called Brother Andrew that he wanted to become a priest.

That could never be, replies the monk. We are made, he informs Shardlake, in the image of God, so anyone with a visible affliction, even a withered limb, could not possibly become a priest. How could Shardlake with his 'great crooked humpback' ever be an intercessor between sinful humanity and the majesty of God?

He then strikes Shardlake across the face and dismisses him with the words 'you crookback churl, get out.' Not surprisingly, the young man was totally cast down. He felt that, if the Church would not have him, he had nowhere else to go.

Then, as he sat on a stile pondering his future, Shardlake claims that Christ spoke to him. The way he describes the experience, which was, for him, a divine intervention, is exactly the same as so many others whom I was to meet writing this book.

'I heard a voice in my head', Shardlake says. 'It came from inside me but was not mine. 'You are not alone, it said and suddenly a great warmth, a sense of peace and love, suffused my spirit … That moment transformed my life. Christ himself had comforted me'.

Then he adds, to me rather convincingly: 'I had never heard that voice before, and though I hoped as I knelt praying that night and in later weeks and years, that I would hear it again, I never have. Perhaps once in a lifetime is all we are given. Many are not even given that'.

That rings true. Many of those to whom I was to talk said that they have only heard that other voice once.

As in Shardlake's case, these 'locutions' seem to arrive in ready-formed phrases which do not seem to come to the recipient through their normal thought-processes. They do not have the quality of a spoken voice, but they can leave the feeling that they have been put into one's consciousness by someone else.

They may suggest a course of action. They may offer an insight into the hearer's or someone else's character. They may warn of difficulties and dangers that lie ahead. They may offer hope and reassurance. Interestingly, those who claim that they have had such thoughts say that the tone in which they arrive can vary considerably. Sometimes, the words and phrases are heard in a gentle and reassuring way, sometimes they are merely informative, sometimes they have a distinctly imperious quality about them.

Frequently, they suggest a course of action which the hearer would not otherwise have considered. A man who confessed to his wife that he had had an affair with a woman at work was told, the very next morning, 'and now tell your mother-in-law!', which he was quite certain did not come from his own thought processes!

These locutions or 'sparks' seem to be altogether different from the sharp stabs of conscience which suddenly pop into our minds and which do not have any spoken quality about them. They are apt to arrive in our consciousness with a dull and depressing thud. The same lack of spoken quality is also, of course, true of the thoughts we have all the time and to which we would attach no kind of divine origin.

So, are these people, from different religious traditions who reckon to have received these so-called 'sparks', in whatever form, simply talking drivel? Are the insights they have been given just the fevered concoctions of their own brains? They might, of course, be nothing more than the product of their social and cultural conditioning, translated into expressions of religious ardour.

But before we conclude that one of those things is what explains them, it is worth observing that many modern psychologists will concede that there is a great deal that we do not yet understand about the workings of our inner selves.

They are by no means entirely sure, for instance, how to describe what our consciousness is, nor are they certain about whether our minds are different from our brains. The term 'explanatory gap' has been coined to describe the fact that purely physical explanations of our minds cannot explain how we feel when we experience things. The truth is that, in this area, there are explanatory gaps all over the place.

Thoughts which come into the mind out of the blue are described by some psychologists as 'orphan thoughts', by others as 'cognitive spam', by others again as examples of human creativity.

So perhaps we should take seriously those who claim to have received these 'sparks', assume that what they are saying could have some vestige of objective reality, accept that perhaps a mysterious divine power can actually communicate with us very directly. It may seem to be a risible notion – and having had such experiences does not turn such people into any kind of spiritual élite, but what they claim is surely worth careful investigation.

After all, if there is a shred of truth in what they believe, I cannot think of anything more important. At the very least, it would open up the possibility that there is a divine power which, far from being a mythical irrelevance, could be the source of a profound wisdom of which, with all our stress and anomie, we are desperately in need.

So, in this book I want to examine the experiences of people who claim to have received, in one form or another, intimations of the divine: and to ask whether, *pace* the Dean, they could not be explained in some other, quite uncelestial way. Are they, on the other hand, experiences that cannot fairly be doubted?

I cannot claim to be entirely objective in my judgements because of experiences I have had myself of what I felt as a guiding hand but, in this book, I want the evidence to speak for itself, to leave readers to make up their own minds. In any case, in these matters there is no such thing as proof, nor ever will be, because God – if there is a God – will always remain the ultimate, unfathomable mystery.

Listening to scores of such people from across the world, one thing at least became abundantly plain. The divine force which they claim to have experienced is neither a heavenly version of the Welfare State, which reckons to iron out the nasty – sometimes brutally nasty – bumps in life's highway, nor does it seek to ensure our so-called 'success' in life, nor even – in the scathing words of Richard Chartres, Bishop of London, 'provide suitable naval officers for our otherwise unmarriageable daughters'.

No, if these people are to be believed, this seems to be a divine power which waits patiently in the shadows for an ear ready to listen, a mind ready to obey – and which can be both exceptionally kind and exceptionally demanding.

But what happens to the people who choose to follow what they are convinced is divine leading? Is it Hallelujah, Hallelujah ever thereafter? Does human error, unhappiness and indeed tragedy vanish from their lives? I just think of Mother Teresa and the fact that she felt that she had lost all touch with God for many years, though she still did what she felt He had called her to do.

If that happened to her, what about the rest of us? These, too, were questions that occurred to me as I went on my journey.

Two

A Life-saving 'Spark'

On my first evening in India, Dr Amit Mukherjee – he of the 'sparks' – did not show up as planned at the guest house in Jamshedpur where I was staying. There was, as it turned out, a very good reason for his absence. Late on the previous evening, he had been operating on a 3-year-old little girl called Jaya, who had two deformed feet. It proved to be one of the most terrifying experiences of his professional life.

When he appeared for breakfast at seven the next morning, he was still reliving the traumas of the night before. The operation, he told me, had begun well enough but then things had started to go wrong, very wrong.

Suddenly, for no obvious reason, Jaya was no longer breathing and no longer had a heartbeat. To revive her, the anaesthetist had twice injected atropine into her heart. Twice, there had been no response.

In that terror-laden silence, both men felt sure that they had somehow lost the child – and that they would have to tell her parents that their daughter had died during what was a quite routine operation. They were both, recalled Mukherjee, very sad and very angry with themselves. How, they wondered, could this have happened to them? 'I was just praying,' he said, 'I didn't know what to do'.

Then, in that moment of panic, he had what he calls 'an arresting thought'. The thought was quite simple, quite unexpected and came with an authority, which demanded obedience: 'Use a larger needle'. That meant taking the atropine from the anaesthetist, something he had never done before in 30 years as a surgeon, fitting a larger needle and injecting the atropine far more deeply into Jaya's heart than they had done so far.

For a few terrifying seconds, nothing happened. Then, to their utter relief, Jaya's heart started beating again. With the aid of a manual resuscitator called an ambu bag, they then tried to start the little girl breathing again. They put a tube down her throat and gave her some oxygen, with the help of a machine.

Suddenly, there was a jerk and Jaya was breathing again. Slowly, painfully, she came back to life. In the end, the operation was a complete success.

That experience, said Mukherjee, as he sipped his breakfast coffee, had made him confident yet again of the presence, somewhere within, of that other voice in which he profoundly believes. 'That', he said, 'was the only thing that saved us last night'.

Was what happened simply a flash of human inspiration when he was *in extenso*, or was it a very timely intervention from the God within? Mukherjee at least has no doubt: such an idea would never normally have occurred to him.

Just as remarkable as the way Mukherjee was able to bring the little girl back to life is the fact that he himself is dying of cancer. His own doctors say that he ought to have been dead the previous summer. Earlier that year they had given him just six months to live. He has a Grade 4 cancer – in the brain, the right lung and the left adrenal gland, and it is spreading, though he claims that 'it doesn't bother me'. He had already had a tumour 'the size of a ping-pong ball' removed from his brain.

Yet he was still carrying on with his normal medical practice, including evening surgeries – and doing so, what is more, with a vitality which I found unbelievable. He behaved like a man in the rudest of rude health. A year after he should have been dead, he was still playing golf, starting at 5.30 in the morning and then going back to begin his morning surgery at 7.30. 'The good Lord', he said with a grin, 'obviously wants me to go on playing golf. That's why I am still alive!'

I had come to that breakfast prepared to be sympathetic and solicitous, to try to help Mukherjee see what is usually called 'the bright side', but it was quite unnecessary. He was on the bright side already.

When he had first been told about the cancer, though, he admits that he had been 'utterly shattered'. Still only 63, he had been planning what he intended to do over the next five, ten years. Now, apparently, he had only six months to live. His doctors had told him that he should quickly put his affairs in order.

One of the things that saved him from total despair was that he had a purpose for such life as he had left. First, there were pressing family duties to fulfil. As a Hindu father, he said, his first responsibility was to find a husband for his daughter before he died. This he had signally failed to do. They had been hunting for a suitable candidate for many months without the least success. Now, a marriage was arranged within a month. Mukherjee clinched the agreement with the other family while he was still in his hospital bed.

'I was even able to give my daughter away', he said. 'Everything went so smoothly it felt as if somebody else was master-minding the whole thing'. The gratitude he felt and which came from inside was indescribable.

Then there were all the projects that he and his friends were involved in as a result of his so-called 'sparks'. One of the most intriguing is the hospital he has set up in a benighted area outside Jamshedpur that did not have one.

Then, there are the remote villages over an hour from the city where once illicit liquor based on fermented rice had taken over communities to such an extent that their farmland was left idle and untilled. He and some of his friends, said Mukherjee, had first become involved when no fewer than 200 people had died after drinking the liquor at a wedding party. They'd felt compelled to do something, and had trekked out there at least 50 times over the years, giving up their precious weekends, in the hope that they could do something to remedy the situation.

And then there were the three-day residential courses which, with the help of the Tata steel company, he and his friends were running for discontented, rebellious, often unemployed young people to give them a new start in life. He wanted me to see something of all these things. It was all arranged.

He also, he added, had a private dream which he hadn't yet spoken about publicly, of founding a hospital in Jamshedpur which would specialise in the treatment of cancer. He wanted to set that project in train before he died.

13

I was astonished that a dying man could still be so passionately committed to the things he cared about, so heedless of his own plight that I wanted to know more of what had made him so; and why he had decided to run his entire life in obedience to the 'sparks' which came to him.

It had all started, Mukherjee told me, when he was a medical student. At that time, he had been very sceptical about the idea of divine direction and he had fierce and inconclusive arguments with a Jesuit priest at Loyola School in Jamshedpur. He had come to the conclusion that such notions were no more than 'the ramblings of a few old folk in weird religious groups'.

Then he'd come across people in Delhi who worked with a body now called Initiatives of Change and who were quite sure that God could communicate with us, particularly in periods of silence which they called 'quiet times'. They didn't drink and they didn't womanise, but they had a kind of joy which Amit found both challenging and infectious.

The idea of a God who 'spoke' wasn't entirely strange to him, partly, he said, because India wasn't like the West. In the West, it was awkward and uncomfortable to touch upon spiritual issues. In India, by contrast, it was the done thing. There was a universal spiritual consciousness in the country, so that talking about things such as quiet times at a dinner party, was no big deal. The other people there might first tell you that you should evolve into meditation, which would take you to even higher realms.

It was also true, he added with a laugh, that Indians could perform a good *puja* (act of worship) in their homes, then go into the office and see nothing wrong in accepting a bribe!

Nonetheless, it riles Mukherjee considerably that India's conquerors – the Mughals and then the British – despised Hinduism and did all they could to wipe it out.

'As a Hindu, he said, 'you were *junglee* – pagan, uncivilised. The common Hindu was not allowed to manifest his religion. Mughal kings slaughtered anyone who was non-Muslim. For 800 years, we were told by both Muslims and Christians that ours was the wrong way, theirs was the right way.

'800 years of counter-propaganda, trying to make us forget the richness that is inherent in us. After all, we come from the richest civilisation the world has ever known – and the people telling us we were wrong came from religions and a thought-process that was only 2000 years old.'

Amit joined the group he'd met in Delhi, though most of them were Christians, because of what he had seen in them and tried out with them the idea of quiet times. They'd sit together in silence, write down the thoughts which came to them and then share them with the others.

In the beginning, he admitted, he had just written down what he thought the others would like to hear. Windy, worthy things such as 'I must be faithful to the Almighty' or 'I need to look deep inside myself' or 'There is a relationship I have to deal with' – although in fact no such relationship existed. 'It was all bunkum', he said. 'There was no spark in it. I did it just to impress the others.'

In any case, he'd thought, 'I don't womanise, I don't drink, so I can't see anything in my life that I need to change'. Then, one day, an Australian in the group suggested that he have a quiet time in which he measured his life against *absolute* moral standards in such things as honesty and love.

'It was the word absolute which pulled me up short', said Mukherjee. 'That was quite a different matter. Then I wrote pages and pages about things that I needed to put right'.

'I'll give you just one example', he went on. 'I was a medical student but, to make some money, I also worked as a sales rep for an engineering firm. I sold many items, to Tata Steel among others. The owner of the business told me that Tata didn't take bribes but that I could invite customers out to meals and send the bills to him.

'I had a large family and we were living in a house with 14 bedrooms – aunts, uncles, cousins – so when I wanted to impress them I'd take them all out for a slap-up meal at the best restaurant in town and send the bill to my boss.

'That was just one of the things which hit me in that time of quiet. I had the thought to apologise to him and return the money, but I knew that that was going to be very difficult.

'There then began a lot of in-fighting inside me. Could I actually do it? When I went to Kolkata to see him, I was still fighting inside. But that other voice can be relentless. It can take away your peace of mind'. But wasn't that just the voice of conscience, I asked? It sounded very much like it. 'No,' retorted Mukherjee, 'my conscience would have said "Good, you admitted doing something wrong". It wouldn't have told me to give the money back.'

'Anyway,' he went on, 'I did tell him, and he was absolutely shocked. He said that he knew all his agents did such things but that he hadn't expected Mukherjee as the son of a senior diplomat – my father was consul-general in Berlin at the time – would stoop so low.'

'I was terribly ashamed,' he said, 'the honour of my family and so on, but I did feel that a great burden had been lifted from my shoulders. I felt so good, I can't tell you. Then, to my amazement, my boss said that he was going to increase my salary, so that I wouldn't need to do such things.'

From that point on, thoughts had come to him constantly from what he had begun to recognise as that other voice. 'I never heard it as a voice, but the thoughts came from outside my normal mental processes and suggested things which I wouldn't normally have considered – "do this", "go there" and "plan in this way". They often suggested things which were the very opposite of formulating plans in a set way!'

He gave one example. He had promised as a young man that, if he succeeded in getting into State medical college – only 200 were accepted out of 25,000 applicants – he would give a year to work in India's deprived villages. After he had qualified, though, he'd gone to Berlin while his father was there, found a job and was having a thoroughly good time.

The only trouble was that, in his time of quiet, that other voice kept saying 'go back, you promised' and it came so persistently 'as if often does' and eventually, it had to be heeded. Mukherjee told me that people would not normally be stupid enough to work in a poor village with no roads and no infrastructure. India's tribal peoples could be dangerous and he'd faced attacks from angry villagers, not to mention encountering leopards, but his two and half years in West Bokaro had been the best of his life.

So slowly, on the basis of actual experience, he had begun to trust that other voice until he became absolutely committed to obeying it wherever it led.

Had that 'voice', though, ever misled him? 'If the results of following a thought are good,' he replied with a grin, 'then I call them sparks. If things don't work out, I call them spooks and say it must have been me speaking! That's happened many, many times I can tell you. Then I take the fatalistic Indian approach and tell myself that it obviously wasn't meant to happen.'

On the other hand, there had been occasions when what, at first, had seem to be spooks had turned out, when pursued, to be sparks. When he'd been working as an orthopaedic surgeon at Tata Tinplate, a young man called Sanat had asked whether he could find a job for him in the company.

He was the first graduate his village had ever produced. Mukherjee's instinct was to say yes, but then the thought came to him to ask whether, since there was no school in Sanat's village, he would consider teaching there to fill that gap.

Sanat was furious. He'd heard Amit was different, he said, but this showed that he was just like all the rest, all talk and no action. What did the surgeon mean by suggesting that he 'take education to his village?' He had no money, no land, how could he even think of it?

Mukherjee assumed that God must have given him the wrong signal and apologised for having made a mistake. When he told his IoC friends, however, they thought it hadn't been such a bad idea though they, too, could not think how to bring it about. They decided to go out to Sanat's village, which meant taking a bus and then cycling. They went 15 times.

At first, there was no response, Sanat refused even to speak to them. But when they continued to visit the village, Sanat's father stepped in. If these people kept coming to the village, how could Sanat be so rude? He would help, he said, by giving his son a plot of land. In the end, Sanat did set up a school and became its headmaster.

Since then, said Mukherjee, there had been hundreds of occasions when such miracles – because that is what he believes them to be – had happened because of that other voice. He'd had to recognise that they were not just coincidences.

The next day, he drove me out to the fledgling hospital he had set up two years before. It is located down a dusty, heavily-rutted track, not far from a large steel works, and has a brick factory right next door. Outside the entrance, there was a heap of lift equipment, wrapped in newspapers.

He introduced me to Dr Mishra, the physician who works at the hospital when he is needed. Mishra said he had not been paid any salary for five months – which, in any case, was 25 per cent less than he could earn outside – but, when he'd seen the children of the area and the poor way in which they lived, he could not help wanting to be of service to them. On the other hand, he did have children at school himself and was praying that the hospital *would* be able to pay him before too long.

The building, said Mukherjee, had once been a local health centre, and was run by a team of dedicated women. They had invited him to join the board and then, with their blessing, he had decided to try to turn it into a proper hospital.

Now, he was the director and did most of his operations there, but took no payment of any kind. In any other hospital, Jaya's parents would have had to pay 30,000 rupees (£500) for her operation, but he had only charged them 5,000 rupees (£85). That was an amount they were able to meet through a government scheme that gives people without health insurance a float of 30,000 rupees (£500) to pay for any treatment they and their family need.

Mukherjee took me on a tour of the hospital. It is simple, clean and trim and now has 32 beds, but there is clearly a long way to go. At first, after he and his friends had decided to go ahead, many people had been unwilling to put up money. It seemed too risky a project to them but then, quite suddenly, that had begun to change after his cancer diagnosis. He found this hard to explain except in terms of encouragement from above.

In a very short time, they had received donations totalling 20,000,000 rupees (£330,000) from large companies in India and America and from many, many individuals who had decided they wanted to help.

Just a week before, a woman from IBM had come to the hospital. She had previously been confused by their requests for instruments and equipment, which was not something her company felt able to help with. Before she came, Mukherjee had been wondering how they would ever be able to afford a good information system to enable them to keep patients' records.

When she asked what they needed and he mentioned an information system, she jumped at the suggestion. Yes, she said immediately, that *was* something they would be happy to help with. 'We will bring in experts from all over the world', she promised, 'and they'll come and spend time with you.' He was expecting them to turn up soon.

'Now, tell me,' said Mukherjee, 'how could anyone have planned all this? Who is doing it? It's not me for sure!' There was no doubt in his mind that a higher power, the one that had given him the idea of a hospital in the first place, was on their side. He believes that all good ideas come from a universal commissioner, and that they should be recognised as divine ideas. Clearly, there was no use telling him either that the timing of the donations was just normal human benevolence in support of a good cause – or that it was another coincidence. As far as he was concerned, it was a sign of God's generosity.

The following day, Amit, his wife Sumita and three of their friends drove me to the villages – Nutundih, Lapunghi and Hurlung – which had once been in the grip of those who made their living from the sale of the liquor known locally as *hadiya*, which did a thriving business in the city as well as the villages. The distilleries had first been set up because many of the men could not find other jobs, and they had soon become the main economy of the villages because the profits were so good and relatively easily made.

The villages can only be reached down a rutted, spine-wrenching track which seems to go on for ever. I marvelled that Mukherjee and his friends had made this journey of 1½ hours at least 50 times in both directions when they could easily have spent their Sundays on the golf course or putting their feet up with their families. Mukherjee himself usually went there by motor bike.

When they'd first gone, he said, 'it was a little more than distilleries and jungle'. There were a dozen largish distilleries and a good many smaller ones – and a minor mafia dealt extremely harshly with anyone who tried to disrupt the trade. The local police were no problem to them, because they took a cut from the profits.

It was a regime of terror, and even some of those marginally involved in the liquor business went in fear of their lives.

Now, all the distilleries have vanished and the villagers –
with a good deal of help from Mukherjee and his friends –
have begun to farm their land again. The fields are no longer
rocky and uncultivated jungle. To help them make a start,
Mukherjee's old company, Tata, was persuaded to give the
villagers three water pumps and dig 40 wells to make sure the
farmers would at least have a regular supply of water.

When we arrived in the village, we were given the warmest
of welcomes from a crowd of people, including a couple
of dozen women between the ages of 15 and 40, who had
come to receive nine sewing machines from Mukherjee's wife
Sumita, the gift of Jamshedpur Women's College of which
she was then principal. (Sumita has since died.)

She also offered the younger women free places in the
college's hostels together with free tuition, so that they could
come and take either four-year graduate classes or vocational
courses. When she asked whether some of her colleagues
might also come and teach in the villages, the answer was a
universal and uproarious 'yes!'

The girls who had been educated, explained Sumita, could
then educate their mothers. There were, she added, women
in the villages who had taken over their households because
their husbands had been drunk so often.

The new head of one of the villages was a woman who
had been beaten by her husband but, after going to the IoC
training centre in Jamshedpur, she had decided to 'light a
candle rather than curse the darkness'. She had become a
graduate and then stood for election. A lot of people had
sneered that she was only a housewife, but she had been
elected anyway.

Mukherjee – who had, incidentally, been up playing golf that morning before we set out – was greeted with cries of welcome in all three villages. Some of the tribal untouchables were particularly glad to see him, because he had invited them for meals in his home, something that would once have been regarded as unthinkable.

When he and his friends had first been to the villages several years before, their reception was anything but friendly. The liquor mafia had sensed that these people from the city might well pose a threat to their business. They didn't know the half of it.

In those early days, Mukherjee had made a particular friend of a man called Budeshwar, who at the time was acting as a guard outside one of the distilleries. After they had gotten to know each other, Amit had told him of his experience of 'the inner voice'. After a while, Budeshwar revealed that he no longer wanted to be involved in the liquor business. His wife and son had left him because they were so afraid of all that was going on.

One of his own relatives, who had somehow heard of his intention, told him he would pay heavily if he dropped out – and actually held a gun to his head.

That was the beginning of a long and painful fight to try to get rid of the distilleries. Amit and Budeshwar sat down often over the course of several years to work out a strategy. Since the local police were hand-in-glove with the liquor producers, he took Budeshwar to meet the police chief. When he heard their story, he drafted in police from other areas, and with them on board organised a raid to smash all the distilleries. He then transferred the local police to other places – permanently.

Budeshwar invited us into his home to meet his wife, Mithila, and their family. She had brought their son back after she was convinced that her husband had had a real change of heart.

'I just did not have peace at home,' confessed Budeshwar. 'We fought among ourselves all the time. And I lived in fear. A jeep would come, and I was afraid that it was the police. I used to bribe them but I was still terribly scared of them.'

When he had first heard of the inner voice, he said, he'd had a great conflict inside himself because of the way he was living. After his first quiet times, he used to share all the good things he'd been doing, not the wrong things – just to give the impression that he was a really good guy. 'I used to fake my story,' he said. Mukherjee entirely understood.

He never spoke of his difficulties with his wife and family, and especially not now that they were no longer living together. Then, after he'd been invited to spend time at Panchgani, the IoC training centre in Maharashtra, he decided that that was no longer good enough and came clean about everything.

So what about the thousands of young people who, funded by money from Tata, have been on the three-day residential courses given by Mukherjee and his friends? I wondered, first of all, why Tata were putting money into programmes of that kind.

'It's certainly nothing to do with profits for the company', said Biran Bhuta, who disburses $35m a year on a variety of what Tata regards as good causes. 'We're a steel company and these youngsters are not consumers of steel. It would be different if Tata was selling hot drinks and biscuits. There is not an iota of vested interest in this'.

No, their philosophy was that, if you were just thinking of the year ahead, you should grow rice. If you had ten years in mind, then you should plant mango trees. If it was 100, you ought to invest in people. Almost two-thirds of Indians were between the ages of 16 and 35 and, if that democratic dividend was not well-channelled, it could easily become a liability.

The majority of the youngsters who came on the courses were tribal people of whom India had 100 million. They were often prey to drugs and alcohol and very often they didn't talk to their parents at all. Young people like that needed help to find a sense of direction in life and he had discovered from first-hand experience that the principles of IoC were a very powerful way of doing that.

All the youngsters who came were given little yellow notebooks in which they could write down the thoughts that came to them when they began to listen to the inner voice. That helped them to become open, to shed their inhibitions and to start thinking about their lives. All the youngsters who came had been affected in some way, 25 per cent of them very deeply.

Tata had sent 200 or so of them to the IoC training centre in Maharashtra, and he wanted to create another Panchgani in the east, because the north-east of India was one of the poorest and most under-developed parts of the country. 'Believe me,' said Bhuta, 'these programmes are no flash in the pan. I'm very confident that they work. Tata does not throw good money after bad!'

'The other thing', he went on, is that there is no religion attached to them. They are religion-agnostic. They're secular and universal, we want to distance ourselves from religion at all costs. They're about simple human values. They're about listening to your own soul'. That seemed like a contradiction in terms for someone who wants to steer well clear of religion, but that is India.

'The company had taken a very sceptical look at IoC before any of the courses were set up,' said Colonel Nair, who runs Tata's Technical Training Centre, 'but we saw that none of their workers was getting paid for what they do here and that the people who came practised what they preached. My secretary fell off her cycle one day and broke her leg. One of the IoC people not only stopped but also took her to hospital. Many people would just have passed by'.

So he'd invited IoC to do sessions with all his new students. Just as on the three-day courses, it was all about listening to the inner voice and then acting on what you'd heard, judged in the light of absolute moral standards.

'Honesty,' he said, 'is very important, because lots of things are now taken for granted in our society – telling small lies, giving and taking bribes, they've become a way of life. To hear that they may not be the right thing to do is truly revolutionary.'

It all sounds thoroughly praiseworthy, but what of the youngsters themselves? After all, it is what has happened to them that matters. Talking to them, it is clear that the inner voice has been far from silent.

Amar is 16. His father, he said, was an alcoholic. He was supposed to run the grocery store which they rent, but he was always getting drunk and so was seldom there. Amar had tried to get him to stop drinking but he wouldn't. Often he'd had to pick up his father who was lying drunk in the road, which made him deeply ashamed. Since the age of 12, he himself had worked eight hours a day in an electronics shop to try to set his father a good example.

None of it had had the slightest effect, so he had decided his father and the whole family could go to hell. He had left home and ceased to take any responsibility for them.

Going on the three-day course had changed all that. He had decided that he had been quite wrong and that he should again take responsibility for the family. He had persuaded the owner of the shop to pay his father monthly rather than daily. His father still took alcohol but nothing like before. They talked together and his father gave him money to help him in running the household. 'He is still my father,' said Amar, 'and I love him.'

At one of Tata's coal-mining plants in Jamadoba, three and a half hours' drive from Jamshedpur, I met a group of sparkling youngsters at a clinic for people suffering from leprosy.

Harprit Kour is 20; she is a Sikh and lives in the village of Sijua. She'd been on the three-day course, she told me, and then spent time at Panchgani. The main lesson of it all was that you could make a big change in the world around you if you were ready to change yourself. She has a quiet time every day and more often when she has a moment to spare.

Her family had once been very poor, but her father now made a good living selling food. Before she'd been on the course, she'd thought that it was the fate of the people they had once lived among to be servants all their lives. The inner voice had told her that that was wrong and that they should have the chance to do something else with their lives, as her own family had done.

So she had decided to start teaching children from a nearby slum without being paid for it. There were 30 of them, many were the children of parents who were servants in her own and other families. They were aged from 4 to 12 and the premises where she taught had been made available by the local Sikh gurdwara (temple). She'd been teaching them for more than two years and they were coming on well. She wouldn't have gone on doing it if she didn't enjoy it so much.

Another impact of the course and Panchgani was that she had become aware that there were many Harprits inside her. Often she had suffered from depression and asked herself why it was only her who was like that? The thought had come to her that she should fight the depression rather than giving in to it – and show her happy face to the world.

Astonishingly, Harprit has also joined an organisation which helps people with sexual and reproductive problems. She'd been taught by a lady doctor and now helps people of both sexes between the ages of 12 and 20. Yes, she tackled all the embarrassing questions they brought to her. 'We call that a brave girl', said one of the leprosy staff who had been listening. So do I!

Mukherjee's 'universal commissioner' seems to have been doing valuable work.

Three

A Now Silent God

The rabbi wanted to hear nothing about universal commissioners, or messages from on high. 'For Jews', he said, 'God is not a divine vending machine. If we have a problem, we wouldn't seek the answer from God. We'd get advice from a rabbi – or a psychiatrist – and having followed the advice, we would never think of blaming God.'

Jonathan Romain is one of Britain's leading liberal rabbis, an accomplished broadcaster and, having been in the job for more than 30 years, he understands what the vast majority of Jews feel about the notion of a God who can communicate with us.

'Are there thoughts that come from God?' he went on. 'We'd regard that as an almost arrogant notion. Why should God take time out to look after little me, to tell me what to do or get me off drugs or whatever? He has much bigger tasks. We do not expect communication from God in that way. We have no sense of having a hotline to the master of the universe. For us, God is a distant presence, not an active interventionist.

'If I said to my congregation here in Maidenhead, that I had had a revelation of some kind from God, they would ask "what on earth is he on about?". It would make me suspect. A member of our congregation once said that God had communicated with her. The response was not "how wonderful!" but "what an idiot!" If someone tells me that God wants them to do this or that, they might call it divine inspiration, but I'd say you're projecting your desires onto Him.'

In Judaism, there were only small and unrepresentative groups – the hasidim – who reckoned to have a daily personal relationship with God. They were rather like Sufi Muslims.

'Most Jews,' Romain went on, 'have never had a personal religious experience. I've never had one myself and it'd be most unusual if I had. It doesn't make any difference. Maimonides (the great Jewish philosopher) said in the thirteenth century that an experience of God was possible, but that most of them were self-induced.

'I'm not writing God out of the script altogether, but He is not one of the *dramatis personae* in my own life. It certainly wasn't God who told me to be a rabbi. I'd never dream of saying that God called me, and I think that goes for all rabbis.'

Many Christians might have much the same reaction as Romain if someone claimed that God had communicated with them, and more than a few might admit that they have had no sort of personal religious experience. Nonetheless, they would probably find Roman's explanation of the Jewish stance extremely odd.

Like the overwhelming majority of Jews, he believes that God finished speaking to human beings at the end of the first

five books of the Hebrew Bible, the Torah. In their Bible, the
book of Job is chapter five. In those five books, Jews are given
no fewer than 613 commandments and that, in Romain's
view, is quite enough to be going on with.

'I'm tempted to say "isn't that enough, mate?" he said. 'It's
hard enough dealing with all those commandments without
receiving further instructions all the time. God had finished
His task by the end of the book of Job. By then, Jews have
been given a template of how they should live and now it's a
question of getting on with it.

'Those first five books are really authoritative. The rest of
the Bible is special, but it doesn't have the same sanctity for
us. Daniel and Ezekiel are a bit suspect and they're not often
read in synagogues. Isaiah? Well, the verses about justice
rolling down are fine, but the stuff about this heavenly being,
no way!'

There may well be, in the Judaic world, several more
nuanced attitudes to the issue of whether God continues to
speak. For example, the former Chief Rabbi, Lord Jonathan
Sacks, explains the Jewish position in similar terms to Romain
but then gives an account of his own personal practice, which
is very different.

'The book of Job,' he said, 'is the last time that God speaks
to human beings. By then, He has said all He had to say to
us. That is it, end of story. He is saying to humanity "I've
said all I have to tell you. Now, you're free to use that wisdom
wisely". So once the book of Job comes to an end, the direct
speech of God to humanity has reached closure. But that is
the record of a conversation which Jews carry with them.
They study it, they sing it, they write commentaries on it,
then they write commentaries on those commentaries.' Since

then, for most Jews, God had remained resolutely silent. They imply that it would be a waste of His time.

'In the books of the Torah,' Sacks went on, 'there is a vast narrative arc, which begins with Adam and ends with Job. Job is the ante-type of Adam. Adam is given everything by God, he is given Paradise, but then he sins. Job has everything taken away and yet refuses to give up his faith. Adam and Job are both, of course, Everyman. God was disappointed by Adam, but Job – who is Adam Mark Two – proves that God was not wrong to have faith in human beings.'

But what about Auschwitz? That, surely, was proof that humanity was *not* to be trusted. Sacks agreed. 'If you ask where was God in Auschwitz, He was there in the words "thou shalt not murder" and "do not oppress the stranger". That's where He was in Auschwitz. When God has spoken and humanity does not listen, there is a tragedy. The religious question is not "where was God in Auschwitz?" He was still there speaking those words, but nobody was listening. To this day, I cannot understand why no one was listening. After Auschwitz, how can anyone have faith in humanity? But why should we blame God?'

Sacks' personal position is very different to the vast majority of Jews, when I asked whether, in his view, God could still speak to us, there was a hesitation and then a qualification.

'Canonically,' he replied, 'there is no subsequent revelation of God which can countermand the Bible. For us, the word of God, which is binding, ended with the canonisation of the Hebrew Bible. Nor do we see God communicating with us as validating religious belief as many Christians do, but some Jewish mystics – the Hasidim – make a discipline of silence, and I personally do that as well.

'I spend a lot of time in silence listening to God. I try to meditate – not many Jews would do that – and, when I sit in silence, there sometimes comes an idea, which distils itself into words. It tells me what I'm doing wrong and what I ought to do to put it right.

'I don't regard it as infallible and, normally, it only translates itself into feelings and sometimes a call. Others might describe that as intuition. But I believe you can hear something that is not a product of your own personality, something that stands outside and says 'this is where you need to be'.

'The most famous line of Jewish prayer is "Hear, O Israel, the Lord our God is one". In my own translation, it is "Listen, O Israel", because I wanted people to understand that hearing God involves a very active form of listening. When Moses says that, he is commanding them to listen to God. I don't regard this as being in the category of revelation, but I do believe that we have to listen to hear the music beneath the noise. That's what I think religious faith is about.'

Sacks, however, is a very unusual Jew in all kinds of ways, and in this in particular. The vast majority believe in a God who has been silent for a very long time, and speaks no longer. He is also a very distant God, and they do not seem to want Him to become less distant.

'For us', said Romain, 'God has two roles. He was somehow the creator of the world and responsible for it. He was also the inspirer of the prophets. So we respect Him and we are grateful to Him for giving life, but we are not asking for His involvement in our daily lives. I do not have a sense of a God who takes a personal interest in me.'

For them, Judaism is a religion of works not faith. 'To be a good Jew,' he went on, 'you do not have to believe in God, you just have to do what He has said. The real heretic is the person who *does* the wrong thing. Our love of God is expressed in doing. The question for us is not what is God doing but what am I doing? There is a rabbinic saying that God has handed over to humans.

'This is not to say that Jews don't believe in God – and in our synagogues there is a light in front of the Torah to show that God is always around – but it is interesting that our beliefs were not formulated until Maimonides did it in the thirteenth century.

'Since Abraham lived in 1800 BC, that means that we waited 3,000 years before we sorted our beliefs out! Our religion is about behaviour, not belief.' Which, I think, perhaps has a distant kinship with St Benedict's remark that religion is about 'truth in behaviour'.

'Judaism,' said Romain, 'is a religion of deed, whereas Christianity often seems to be essentially a religion of creed. I was once a judge in the Times Preacher of the Year competition and the rabbis who spoke always talked about practical issues – the Jewish attitude to things such as cancer, abortion, charity. All the Christians, on the other hand, used their sermons to talk about belief'.

What, though, were the characteristics of his silent, distant God? Was He, for example, a God of love? 'That,' replied Romain, 'is an almost irrelevant question. The Jewish question is ' "What does He want from us?" He wants *us* to love, that is what matters'.

When it came to prayer, they didn't expect to make a connection with Him in any immanent sense. They had no sense of *shekinah*, of a divine presence. You might get a sense of satisfaction because you had prayed, but that was all.

'There is a Hebrew word for prayer, *lehitpallel*', he said 'and its primary root means "to judge oneself". So, for us, prayer is not petitioning or haranguing God, but a way of looking at our own lives and asking ourselves "Are we up to the mark?"'

Of course those prayers were addressed to God, but they were like a letter which did not expect a response. The fact that they had written the letter and posted it was what mattered.

Jews were supposed to pray three times a day, but it was rare to find a Jew praying privately and they didn't have any practice of impromptu prayer.

'Once when I first started doing things on the radio,' Romain recalled, 'the interviewer said at the end of the programme "Would you like to end with a prayer?" and I was totally flummoxed. I gawped at him, there was a stunned silence and, in the end, I muttered something about "Bless us with Your mercy'. I couldn't just say "We don't do that", could I?'

Two of Romain's cousins died in Auschwitz and his mother Gabrielle escaped on the Kindertransport, but she never talked about it. The Holocaust of course raised for Jews the question of God's apparent silence and many did not know how to explain it.

'If you regarded God as a watchmaker,' said Romain, 'you might think that, having made the watch, He just let it tick on. If, on the other hand, you saw God as someone who intervened in human history, then – hang on! – why didn't He intervene?'

One of the answers to these profound puzzles was that it was a time of God's silence, a silence which was entirely in character since He had already laid down the spec for how Jews were meant to live, and so had stopped speaking long ago.

Since most Jews do not believe in a God who intervenes in that way, they perhaps should not have been surprised that He did not step in. According to Sacks, He had already stepped in through the words He had spoken in the Torah.

Four

The Dean's Story

Martyn Percy, the Dean of Christ Church, Oxford, is a rather unusual Dean. To begin with, that is not his birth name. Having been born, in Blackburn, he took the surname of the couple, Roy and Sylvia, to whom his mother handed him over for adoption. He arrived dressed in little girl's clothes, which suggested to his adoptive parents that he might have an older sister, which proved to be the case, as he later discovered.

He has had a distinguished career in the Church of England. He is credited with doing a splendid job at Cuddesdon, perhaps the best-known of the C of E's theological colleges, where he was Principal for ten years before being invited to become Dean at Christ Church.

Percy does not look like the archetypal Dean. He is not tall and imposing; he ambles down the aisle in the cathedral, which also doubles as the college chapel, looking preoccupied as if he were dwelling in a different world. But he has a fine mind, great inner warmth, and a lively sense of humour. He is not so foolish as to think too highly of himself.

His beginnings may be remarkable, but it is his spiritual experiences which have brought him to where he is. He has had three epiphanies, which the dictionary describes as 'moments of great and sudden revelation' but which Percy prefers to call 'supra-manifestations – or surprising intimations of the divine, or even God's ambushes – all beyond human reasoning or control'. Percy believes in a 'God of surprises'.

To my mind, his trinity of experiences illustrates perfectly three of the ways in which that other 'voice' – in all its forms - can make its appearance in people's lives.

Percy speaks about these experiences somewhat reluctantly, partly because they are so personal. He is also concerned that, by owning them, there is a risk of claiming a bogus spiritual eminence, giving the impression that he thinks God singles people out for divine favours not granted to others.

He believes no such thing, and shares these experiences only because he is grateful for what they have meant to him and because he wants to bear witness to the way - or rather *a* way – that the infinitely mysterious God seems to have dealt with him. He prefers to see epiphanies as 'open and opaque' - a way of reading what might very well be the hand of God interacting with our own lives. But like most descriptions of reality, it can only be interpretative, not absolute.

The first of these experiences took place when Percy was 16 and at school in North London. It wasn't particularly dramatic and took time to come to fruition but was, nonetheless, utterly compelling and has shaped his entire future.

Though he had always liked the idea of learning, he hadn't found anything in his school work that really inspired him. In fact, he was so uninterested that he says he'd virtually taken two gap years off while still at the school.

Since both of his parents had left school at 14, and nobody in the family had ever been to university, Percy was keen to leave school and get some kind of job. His parents, however, insisted that he took a careers test first.

It was an idea towards which he was decidedly cold, but he did as he was told. When the people who'd talked to him reported their conclusions, it initially made matters worse. The letter said that, while Martyn had not seemed much engaged in the process – which was putting it mildly – on the basis of what they had found out about him, they thought he might in later life become a teacher or a lecturer – or a cleric.

A *cleric*! Percy was confounded. 'I could cope with the idea of becoming a lecturer or teacher, but I couldn't think of anything more 'nerdy' than becoming a priest. Don't forget, I was a sulky, angry teenager with all the hormones buzzing around, and I was not a conformist'. He had felt that the interview would be a waste of time, and so it had apparently proved.

That, however, was not the end of the story. It was, he says, like a slowly exploding bomb. Over the course of the next fortnight, a conviction grew in him that, if he did anything else than become a cleric, it would be less than the best. Perhaps this had something to do with the fact that his parents had raised him in their own evangelical Christian tradition.

In any event, as the days went by, though he didn't hear an actual voice, there might just as well have been one. It was, he says, 'like a voice which shouted inside and which gradually gave me an incredibly strong inner sense of calling. At first I was very angry with that 'voice'. It made me uncomfortable. I hated the sense that, if I obeyed, my life was already mapped out. Here was this 'voice' effectively saying 'I've got a plan for the rest of your life', at the very moment when I wanted a sense of freedom.

'The process was a bit like breaking in a horse. Jesus's words "take my yoke upon you, you'll find the burden is light", came to mind. Becoming a cleric wasn't what I wanted and in terms of my human ambition it certainly wasn't the kind of thing you'd have taken aim for. On the other hand, I increasingly felt that the yoke would be light.'

David Jenkins, the former Bishop of Durham, had argued that, if God did ever speak to us, it would always be negotiable given that He is a God of love, but his growing sense of calling didn't feel at all negotiable to the young Percy. All he knew was that doing anything else would be less. He didn't feel completely trapped but he did feel cornered – and after a couple of weeks, there came a moment of acceptance, of surrender.

The upshot was that he changed tack, stayed on at school and signed up for three A levels – Ancient History, English and RE – and loved working for them. After that, he says, ordination seemed inevitable, but he still wonders whether, if he had said no, God would just have walked away and left his life to take its own, humanly determined, way.

Percy's second epiphany was rather more startling. He had left school, been to university in Bristol, done a PhD in London and a Masters in education at Sheffield University. Then, a friend who had become his spiritual counsellor, advised him that, if he were going to be ordained, he had better do something out in the world first. If the call he spoke about really was from God, the friend added, it would still be there in five years' time. So Percy spent four years working for different publishers, and 'moonlighted' a bit for the BBC.

During all that time, he says, the call he had heard as a 16-year-old never left him alone for a single day. It was like trying to run with a powerful elastic band drawing him back all the time. After four years, he had become so restless that he simply couldn't stay in publishing any longer.

He consulted a close spiritual adviser, who listened to him and then went to his front door, locked it and put the key in his pocket. 'You're obviously ready to have your call tested', he said, 'so I'm going to ring the Director of Ordinands in the diocese, and you can't leave until I've done it'.

Nine months later, after he'd been through 'the usual hoops' ending in a selection conference, Percy was asked to go to Durham for ordination training. He didn't want to be there, it was too far away and he felt as if he were being forced to go north.

The fact that his first interview in Durham didn't go at all well simply added to his confusion and uncertainty. Feeling thoroughly disturbed, he stomped off into the cathedral and had a furious verbal argument with God. He acknowledged that although, by this time, despite all his doubts, he had an almost overwhelming inner sense that he ought to come to Durham, he still wanted to know why?

Then, he recalled, there came 'this strong inner voice, which was audible in my head and in no way external'. It said: 'Come'.

After lunch, there was a second interview, this time with the college's principal. He said that they would very much like Percy to come and that he was quite sure he would enjoy his time there. Percy recalls replying, rather ungraciously, that he wasn't at all sure that he would.

When he came out of the interview, though, he saw – on a board – photographs of all the other ordinands, perhaps 40 of them. A number, of course, were women. When he came to the photograph of the woman who turned out to be his future wife Emma, there came not a voice but a very clear thought which he says was 'that's her, that's your wife-to-be'.

He didn't seek her out, but later that day Emma spoke briefly to him. Things proceeded, in some ways, rather slowly. It took a month or so before they both realised that they had fallen in love. One day, they went for a walk together and Emma said it first – 'I think we are in love'. Percy responded that he felt just the same. Emma asked what he thought they should do about it and he replied: 'Get married'. Nine months later, they did.

He came to Christ Church in 2014, and his third epiphany was of a very different kind. 'I'd first come here to preach nine years ago', he recalled, 'and I remember sitting in the Latin Chapel of St Frideswide preparing myself for the service when, suddenly, I felt overcome. I was actually shaking and I wondered if I was having a religious experience. It was so unusual that I made a rough mental note of it.

'At that time I had not remembered my baptismal certificate. I only discovered after that service in Christ Church that, when my parents were having some legal difficulty in adopting me, they took me to their nearest church, near Liverpool, which happened to be dedicated to St Frideswide – and I was baptised there. I thought, 'Good grief, that was St Frideswide too!'

'Then came the invitation to become Dean. I realised that, if I accepted, I would be a kind of spiritual successor of the first Prior of St Frideswide. It felt like an extraordinary moment'. It does indeed. The cathedral where Percy now preaches includes significant parts of the Priory of St Frideswide which was set up in 1122 by Gwymund, chaplain to Henry I. It is also the place where St Frideswide, an abbess and princess of the seventh century, set up her monastery.'

'I think that there was an inner voice,' Percy went on, 'but this time it was a voice of a different kind, and my response to it had to be rather different.'

So, with the benefit of hindsight, what does Percy make of these experiences? Awe, gratitude and wonder, certainly, but with no doubt about where the different 'voices' or impulsions came from? The interesting thing to Percy is that each time he had one of his epiphanies, he did not see himself as being in 'a seeking mode'. Like the slave captain, John Newton, he was 'found' when he wasn't even aware that he was lost. God seems to have intervened without him either seeking or willing it.

For Percy, these 'epiphanies' are opaque. They are, he says, like the 'signs' in John's gospel. They point beyond themselves to a higher reality that can't be grasped. The signs still require reading, and if you choose to follow them, graft. The epiphanies we think we have are not straightforward. They leave us, as God does, with space to relate, doubt, and even refuse them. But that they are there, he is not in doubt. That said, 'for every single time we think we hear God's voice clearly, and it turns out that way, we are probably wrong for the other ninety-nine times. So each sense of any epiphany needs careful sifting and discernment, and perhaps some interpretation too. They are not straightforward.'

Percy adds a number of other caveats and qualifications. He believes that these epiphanies can exist, but has little time for the notion that God had a pre-ordained plan for him, or indeed, for any of us. To him, the very idea suggests a kind of spiritual 'class system', where there are those in one tier who receive divine favours – and often regard themselves as 'the chosen' – and a tier of people who are not so privileged.

He knows all too well, from his pastoral work, that there are many people who cry out for God's help and don't seem to receive it – at least in the form they want – and end up believing that they simply haven't been heard; others again who are convinced that God has spoken to them – about relationships, money and health - and are shattered when the outcome is quite different from what they had been led to expect. We have to be very careful, says Percy, when we think we have heard God speaking to us. We always need to apply discernment and testing – measuring what we think we have heard against the standards of the scriptures and taking the advice of trusted friends – before leaping to any such conclusions.

To him, it is all evidence of a God whose activities can seem to be utterly random, a God who may be infinitely loving; but who is also unbiddable, unpredictable and impossible to fathom. This is the God who writes in poetry and symbols, not just on the wall or on tablets of stone, in clear prose.

That is why he believes in what he calls a 'fuzzy' God and why he holds to what he calls 'a broad but not liberal' faith. He loves poets such as Donald Davie and often turns to them to express more nearly what he feels – and to one poem in particular – Davie's 'Ordinary God':

> *'Do you believe in a God*
> *who can change the course of events*
> *on earth?'*
> *'No, just*
> *the ordinary one.'*
> *A laugh,*
> *but not so stupid: events*
> *He does not, it seems, determine*
> *for the most part. Whether He could*
> *is not to the point; it is not*
> *stupid to believe in*
> *a God who mostly abjures.*
>
> *The ordinary kind*
> *of God is what one believes in*
> *so implicitly that*
> *it is only with blushes or*
> *bravado one can declare,*
> *'I believe'; caught as one is*
> *in the ambush of personal history, so*
> *harried, so distraught.*
>
> *The ordinary kind*
> *of undeceived believer*
> *expects no prompt reward*
> *from an ultimately faithful*
> *but meanwhile preoccupied landlord.*

That, for Percy pretty much says it all. Thankfully, in his case, the landlord does not seem to have been entirely preoccupied.

I asked Percy if he could ever deny the reality of his own personal experiences? 'If you ask, do I think I can hear a voice?, he replied, 'Yes I do. If you ask was it an inner voice, yes, it was. If you ask whether I believe it was God speaking through that inner voice? Yes, I do. Hearing and sensing in this way can be likened to becoming attuned to a different sound. It can feel like an unmediated voice, which seems to come from nowhere and yet it comes from within. I don't mind at all if you want to call it a voice from Heaven.'

He continued, 'All of it, of course, is completely unknowable. There is no rhyme or reason about it, but it works because there are so many things in this world that we cannot explain. Shakespeare's comment on the fact that reason can only take you so far – Horatio's observation in Hamlet that "there are more things in heaven and earth than are dreamt of in your philosophy" – is entirely appropriate.

'Saint Augustine talks about our mind being in two halves. The lower mind is all rationality and reason – how to drive a car, how to make a pudding. The upper half, which he calls nous, or intuitive apprehension, is for communication or communion with God. It is not a physiological thing but an area of spiritual discernment.

'C. S. Lewis described those things as "spiritual inklings" – being able, somehow, to see round the corner before getting there. It is also something like the Buddhist notion of getting in touch with how things *truly* are – making contact with the reality of yourself and the world around you.'

He believes that hearing God speak is a good deal more ordinary and widespread than you might have thought. He suspects that it happens to everyone, though not everyone realises it. It was, he said, perfectly possible to ignore God, just as you could ignore the very air you breathe and take for granted. But when those who had been starved of that air started to breathe it again, they had some extraordinary experiences.

To hear that voice – whether we spoke of it as a literal hearing or an inner hearing – simply requires that we pay attention to our inner landscape, listen to our spiritual intelligence, 'what used to be called wisdom'.

It was about being ready to acknowledge that there is a gap between perceived reality and intuition, something far beyond logic. It was well beyond rocket science. Of course that didn't mean that God had a voice-box, a tongue, a set of lungs. It was impossible to describe, or limit, God. So it was important that we didn't try and replace the unfathomable mystery of God with 'facts'.

Percy has the unusual distinction of being the only living theologian named and quoted in Dan Brown's bestseller, *The Da Vinci Code*. In Chapter 55, Percy is quoted by the character Teabing, as saying 'the Bible did not arrive by fax from heaven'; he meant that even in the scriptures, there is poetry, analogy, signs, symbols, metaphors and histories - all of which have multiple ways of being read.

'The Bible', he said, is not just a bunch of facts, written by God and faxed to us. When Jesus wrote, he scribbled in the sand. We don't know what God looks like. We don't even have a physical description of Jesus in the Gospels. Once you have received a real sense of that inner voice, however, it did require you to be responsive, discerning, testing - and perhaps obedient.' That rang a loud bell for me. That has been my own experience, as I shall come to later.

I asked him if he had been glad that he had been responsive to these 'inklings'. 'Yes,' he replied, 'though some days are gladder than others. But it's much deeper and far wider than "glad". But if you ask whether other things might have been more fulfilling, the answer is no.' That, too, has been my own experience.

And what was the Dean going to be doing in the days ahead, I asked? Percy smiled. He recalled Woody Allen's jocular quip: 'How do you make God laugh? Tell him your future plans.'

Given that he believes in a God of surprises, all we can do in his view is be faithful to the past and to the fullness and loving presence of God in the here and now.

'God abides with us always and never leaves us or forsakes us. The days ahead for you and me and everyone else will be as it is now – all about finding God in the moment and working out His will for our lives'.

Five

Oracles, but not God

There didn't seem to be much point in going to Dharamsala, the Dalai Lama's North Indian hillside home since 1959. All my knowledgeable friends, including two men who have spent a good deal of time with His Holiness, were sure that there would be no Buddhist of any eminence to see me at the time I had planned to be there. They'd all be either on holiday or travelling. It was such a pity, they said, that I wasn't going at a better time.

One of my friends, Alex Norman, who is the director of the Dalai Lama's Centre for Compassion in Oxford, had said that the two people he'd liked me to have met in Dharamsala were Tendzin Choegyal, the Dalai Lama's younger brother, and the Venerable Lhakdor, a monk who runs the National Library of Buddhist Works. Unfortunately, there was very little chance that either would be there, but I could at least stay at Kashmir Cottage, a guest house which Choegyal and his wife Rinchin own and run.

The prospects didn't sound at all good, but the flight from Kolkata via Delhi was booked; I didn't want to waste the money and, given the lack of any obvious alternative, I decided to go anyway.

The only mildly reassuring thought I'd had – I had no idea whether it was a spark or a spook – was 'leave it to me'. The implication seemed to be that, if I went to Dharamsala, it might not be a complete dead loss. And so it proved. I had expected three rather unfruitful days. I could not have been more wrong.

Before I left for India, I'd done a little preparatory digging, so that I didn't arrive in Dharamsala with no idea of how Buddhists might respond to the notion that God might be able to communicate with us in some way – though I knew that they didn't believe in a God of any kind.

Having met the Dalai Lama briefly a couple of times, in London and then in Delhi, I found it hard to believe that the response would be entirely negative. Indeed, Alex Norman had told me that while His Holiness would resist the idea of a personal God, he did reckon to have had one mystical experience in a Christian context. He had thought a statue of the Virgin Mary he'd seen in London had actually smiled at him – which he had found quite astonishing, not surprisingly, since he is the least gullible of men.

Not all Buddhists are quite so instinctively oecumenical. Amaro Bhikku, an Englishman who is abbot of the Amaravati monastery near Hemel Hempstead, will have none of the notion of a God who can communicate with us. The idea of being talked to by what he called 'the ultimate reality' was, he said, 'total anathema to Buddhists'.

What Buddhists believed was that, when you were faced with difficult decisions in life, you should take time to reflect and consult your own mind about the best way to handle the issue. You were *not* asking God to enlighten and guide you.

When Buddhists took time to reflect, he went on, what they were doing was drawing on their connectedness to everything in the universe, which was far more intimate, far closer, than the thinking mind could articulate. You were drawing on your own oracle, your own guide. 'My own wisdom', said Bhikku, 'puts itself into a voice which is quite recognisable, but it comes from my own mind'.

To help Buddhists in this process of reflection and discernment, there was help at hand. In the northern Buddhist world – Tibet, China and Korea – there were beings, role models rather like Christian saints – who could help them in their search for right judgement.

These were the bodhisattvas, beings who had vowed to become Buddha-like, not for their own sake but for the sake of others. Each of them was the symbolic embodiment of a particular virtue or area of operation. There was, for example, a bodhisattva of medicine, Bhaisajyaguru, who represented an incarnation of healing in all its aspects.

The best-known, though, were Manjushri, the bodhisattva of wisdom; Avalokitesvara, the bodhisattva of compassion or love, who concerned himself with the little sufferings of everyday; and Vajrapani, the bodhisattva of power. A fourth bodhisattva, Tara, was the epitome of the female aspect of compassion.

Occasionally, these bodhisattvas manifested themselves in human form – the Dalai Lama was believed to be the embodiment of the bodhisattva of wisdom – but more commonly they were seen in the form of painted images, and Buddhists would pray to those images as a Christian might pray to an icon.

Bodhisattvas, said Bhikku, were able to inspire you, to guide you and, in some sense communicate with you. Were they perhaps, I wondered, a Buddhist version of that other voice? How real were they, I asked? 'How real is God?' replied Bhikku.

In the southern Buddhist world – Thailand, Sri Lanka and Burma – there was no belief in such intercessory deities, he went on – but the same process of reflection went on without named beings such as bodhisattvas.

Instead, Buddhists in those countries sought help and inspiration by doing partita chanting. That, he said, was really a way of sending out an SOS to all the forces of good in the universe, asking them to show up and lend a hand – or so that the best of yourself, your best qualities were summoned up as you chanted.

That left me wondering exactly how bodhisattvas or 'the forces of good in the universe' actually communicated with those who turned to them for help. Was it all in the end down to your own mind, your own wisdom? In Oxford, I met a Tibetan monk, Tenzin Damcheo, and put the question to him.

'Maybe they do it through their mobiles!' he replied with a laugh. The Dalai Lama is by no means the only Tibetan Buddhist with a lively sense of humour.

There were many instances, he went on, when a bodhisattva had actually spoken to a disciple who was praying to them. One of the best-known examples was that of Atisa, an Indian Buddhist master of the tenth century, who believed he had received guidance from Tara, the female bodhisattva.

She had made a prophecy to him, which he had heard within himself in a moment of revelation: 'If you go to Tibet, you will have a shorter life, but you will do a great work for the truth there.' At first, Atisa had not been willing to go, but Tara kept saying 'Go! Go!'to him. 'It was like Moses going up the mountain and hearing God's voice,' said Damcheo. There were many lamas – monks of great wisdom – who had had such visions and been spoken to in that way.

But that, Damcheo went on, was 'not a cup of tea for everyone. If a fox tried to jump like a horse, it would break its back.' Until he himself had reached 'the higher realisation' – and there were 37 stages of enlightenment in Buddhism – the bodhisattvas were not going to communicate with him. It depended on your level of devotion and he didn't have the proper level.

He'd been a monk for 17 years but still had great difficulties – attachment to his family and friends, anger, ignorance, desire. Those things stopped him from being enlightened. What did he feel angry about, I asked? 'My computer', he replied laughing. 'I keep having to press the refresh button!'

And so, somewhat apprehensively, to Dharamsala. In the moments before we landed, we had an all-too-brief glimpse of the majestic sweep of the Himalayas – and then it was upward, ever upward, along steepling, often crumbling roads to Kashmir Cottage, 6,000 feet up on the mountainside.

Hairpin bends, great chasms on one side, deep ditches and drains on the other. Noticing my alarm at what seemed like very close shaves, the taxi driver tried to reassure me. They never, he said, had accidents on these roads. The influence of Buddhism was perhaps stronger than I had imagined.

My only contact in Dharamsala, a friend of a friend whom I'd never met before, was Tashi, who turned out to be a charming student of Tibetan musical instruments – various types of fiddle bow, the lute and the dulcimer as well as monastic instruments such as cymbals and conch shells.

He was, said Tashi, a human being first, a Buddhist second and he wanted to die 'smilingly' having done everything he should have done. He had managed to arrange only one interview for me – oh dear, I thought, that doesn't sound good – but it was with the first of Alex Norman's wish-list, the Venerable (Geshe) Lhakdor – director of the national library.

Lhakdor was going on his travels very soon, said Tashi, but he would be happy to see me, twice if need be, before he left. We set out immediately for the library. It is in the village of Macleodganj, named after a British officer. On the way, we passed something called the Pain-Free Physiotherapy Clinic, a promise that certainly did not match my own experience of physios.

Lhakdor was brisk but welcoming. A heavily-built man in his sixties, he has been a monk for 40 years and is a considerable scholar. He also has an abundant sense of humour. Was there, I asked him, any resonance at all in Buddhism for the notion of that other voice?

Oh, there were so many voices inside us, he replied – anger, frustration, compassion, so many. And then there was the voice which came through you but was not your voice, though that didn't happen to everybody. That sounded rather familiar. What came next certainly wasn't.

To begin with, said Lhakdor, there was a Tibetan tradition which went back 1,200 years and enshrined the belief that there were human beings who could act as mediums through whom the voice of an oracle, a higher spiritual power, could speak. They had, of course, to be special people with very pure minds. It was like the moon. If you wanted to see the moon reflected in water, the water had to be very pure. So not all water could reflect it – and the Geshe roared with laughter.

He was clearly not talking, as Abbot Bhikku, had done, of Buddhists being able to access their very own oracle. There were, said Lhakdor, very few oracles – which he defined as 'creatures who were sentient but formless' – they could be either positive or negative and they had to be invoked to speak. Their answers obviously depended on what you asked them.

Nor did the oracle manifest itself just because a Buddhist had been mulling over, in meditation, some particular difficulty or predicament. For example, when the Tibetan State oracle – known as the Nechung Oracle – was consulted, there was a great ceremony in the monastery up the hill.

The medium, or Kuten, whose task it was to make contact with the oracle, was always the same monk. During the ceremony, he was dressed in an elaborate costume topped by a robe of golden silk brocade. He also put on a kind of harness that supported four flags and three victory banners. The whole outfit weighed well over 70 pounds and, when the Kuten was not in a trance, he could hardly manage to walk in it. Once in a trance, said Lhakdor, he was able to jump and dance.

As the ceremony went on, and the medium's trance deepened, his helpers gave him a headdress that today weighs 30 pounds. In the past, it had weighed as much as 80 pounds. It all sounded like hard work. After the ceremony was over, said Lhakdor, the medium – not surprisingly – often needed a prolonged period of convalescence.

Somehow, said Lhakdor, the Kuten managed to enter into the consciousness of the deity and his whole body became transfigured. When the oracle had entered him, the medium's own capacities faded away and he was overpowered by the oracle's spiritual power. The same sort of thing happened in ordinary life, said Lhakdor, when we were struck dumb in the presence of a very powerful person.

When the oracle spoke to the medium, he spoke in his own realm, his own language – 'like dogs which bark but understand each other' – but his words, rendered into Tibetan by the Kuten, came out of the medium's mouth. The Dalai Lama was convinced that the oracle had helped guide him when he was trying to escape from the Chinese in 1959.

Of course they didn't bother to consult the State oracle on minor issues, said Lhakdor, only when something about the future of Tibet had come up. Even then, it was a last resort. The Dalai Lama would first try to come to a decision on the basis of common sense, and then he'd talk with his Cabinet. Only if a solution still wasn't in sight did they turn to the oracle.

That, though, said the Geshe, was not the only way that Buddhists could become aware of a voice which was not their own. All the great bodhisattvas could communicate with those who prayed to them and sought their help.

'If you make a special prayer for a long time,' he said, 'and you really long to become wiser, and even after meditating you felt nothing was any better, you can visualise Manjushri and he may appear to you or communicate with you in some other way'.

'It's as if you've been thinking about your girlfriend for a long time because she's in New York. As you think about her, she will become very clear in your mind and you'll even begin talking with her, imagining her responses. That's almost like a voice'.

If I was still trying to understand what bodhisattvas were, he went on, there were two possibilities and it didn't really matter which I chose. The first was that bodhisattvas such as Manjushri may never have existed in human form, they were just representations of wisdom or compassion. Buddhists portrayed them in paintings and, when they saw the image of Manjushri, they became more eager to emulate him.

'The other possibility,' he said 'is that there *was* a Manjushri who had actually lived once upon a time. The aim is the same, to develop the kind of wisdom that he is said to have practised. It doesn't matter that you have never seen him. In your own case as a Christian, you have never seen God, but it doesn't mean that your image of Him won't benefit you in some way.'

Buddhists might not believe in the idea of a soul, but they did believe in conscience – 'almost like soul-custodian', and he roared with laughter. If you didn't have vigilance and introspection, then you didn't have any idea whether what you are doing was bad or good.

'That,' said Lhakdor, 'is why meditation is so important. Your thoughts are like ceaseless ripples on water. Your ears listen, your eyes see, your tongue is tasting, your nose is smelling. You are bombarded with information, so you need to discriminate, to decide which thoughts you should welcome and say 'please come, have a cup of tea!' and to which you should say 'go away, get lost!" Meditation was not just sitting in the temple and closing your eyes!'

People were always insisting that we had to know exactly when the world began and who created it, but how were we even to know exactly when and how that had happened and who was responsible? If the reply was God, even that could not be the complete answer. It only invited the question 'so who created God?' The final result of it all was just more questions.

'Since so many people were overcome by suffering and needed our help, we shouldn't waste our time on dry philosophical questions like that'. And again the Geshe roared with laughter.

Why, I wondered, did Tibetans laugh so much – and about the most profound things? It was, Lhakdor replied, partly to do with their nature and history. 'We lived in nature, in a land as big as Western Europe, we were not troubled by an excess of population and, when you saw other human beings, you felt very happy. You didn't mind where they came from.'

The second thing was the teaching of the Buddha, who said that the solution for the many ills we faced was not external accumulation – wealth, family and so on. The most important thing was your mental outlook. He said that we should seek to cultivate an outlook that would help us in all weathers. The Buddha had also told them to take life as lightly as possible.

There had always, I said, been one thing about Buddhism which puzzled me; the idea that much of our suffering was caused by our attachment to things and people. The suggestion seemed to be that we should therefore avoid all attachments, and I wondered where that left the love we felt for our family and friends?

The Geshe laughed. 'There is a European saying,' he replied, 'that "love is not how many times you touch each other but how many times you reach each other"''. That conveys the right message. The ordinary notion of love is that we should hug, possess, touch and make all the right declarations, especially during the honeymoon' – and he roared with laughter yet again.

Ordinary love was good, but it was still alloyed. A person might say 'I love you so much' but what they really meant was 'I will love you as long as you love me'. That was called conditional love. We sometimes called it business love.

Buddhists believed in unconditional love; that you shall love someone not because they were your relative or your friend, but because you knew that they, like other people, wanted happiness, but that they were often suffering, and needed to be taken care of.

Why, you might ask, he went on, should we take care of others and not just ourselves? The Buddhist answer was that just taking care of yourself was very short-sighted, because the secret of long-lasting peace was to look after other people.

So, of course, Buddhism did not exclude love for family and friends, but you should not want anything for it. You should be focussed on the fact that all those around you wanted happiness and not suffering. Ordinary love, expecting something in return, was okay but it was not the best.

When I arrived back at Kashmir Cottage, there was great excitement. To everybody's surprise, Tendzin Choegyal was coming back later that same day – his Holiness tomorrow. The hotel receptionist ran down to my room to say that

'Mem' – Choegyal's wife Rinchen Khanda – would like to ask me why I wanted to talk to her husband. He'd be very tired after two months' continuous travelling abroad and he might just want to go to bed.

I told Rinchen that the title of the book was likely to be *That Other Voice* and that appeared to ring an immediate bell. She said: 'I'm moved by that title, it speaks to me.' So many of us spent our lives listening to all the frivolous voices in our head, and either missed or ignored the more profound voice which was there within – which you might call conscience. There was just a hint in the way she spoke that she might believe that there was more to it than that.

Anyway, that other voice was the reason why, for the last 20 years, she had been working to get Tibetan nuns educated. So many of them had had no choice in the first place and did not even know why they had become nuns.

She was now trying to care for 700 of them and had had help from the West. His Holiness had supported the idea from the beginning. I told Rinchen that I'd met His Holiness briefly twice – and, in my naïve and impertinent way – had then asked the Almighty what He made of the Dalai Lama? The answer was firm and immediate: 'He is one of my own!' As far as I was concerned, that was the other voice speaking.

One did, though, said Rinchen, have to be very careful in obeying what came from that other voice. Cross-checking with friends was a great thing in Buddhism. The Buddha had said that we should not dutifully respect his word but, instead, be like the wise goldsmith who tested his material nine times before starting to make anything.

Anyway, she said, she'd do her level best to try to persuade her husband. An hour later, the receptionist came down again and said that Choegyal and his wife would like to see me for supper.

The evening started disastrously, because of my clumsiness. Tashi had given me a folded white cloth to give to Choegyal and his wife. The trouble was that I didn't unfurl it, but presented it to them still rolled up. It was supposed to be like flowers, explained Choegyal, a little tartly. Thankfully, that *bétise* served to break the ice instead of ruining the evening.

While Rinchen prepared supper, Choegyal and I talked. He has a face which has something of the Dalai Lama's about it – though he wears spectacles and has the lively eyes of a natural nonconformist. Like most aristocratic Tibetans from the 1950s onwards, he had been sent to a missionary school – St Joseph's in Darjeeling, so that he'd receive a first-class education. Thereafter, he had led a rather chequered life and spent time in the Indian army before becoming his elder brother's private secretary for eight years. Now, they usually travel together.

If the Dalai Lama were not such a joker himself, Choegyal would be the joker in the pack. 'When we were going through passport checks in New York,' he said, 'a man asked how many there were in our party. I replied, "Eight, but only one is working!" – and the man burst out laughing.'

He also has a profoundly serious side, as I soon found out. He has a far more rigorous conception of meditation than those who regard it as little more than a technique for restoring inner calm. 'It is not just a pain-killer', said Choegyal. 'It's much more like going to the gym. It's a vehicle through which you can analyse what is troubling you – and make you healthier mentally as well as physically.'

The heart of it – what he called 'the beef of the story' – was to help you get in touch with reality and then find release from 'the prison of attachment.' He'd been a boarder at St Joseph's - and discovered there that it was much the same in all the great religious traditions.

When, for example, Jesus said that it was easier for a camel to pass through the eye of a needle than for a rich man to enter the Kingdom of God, it was attachment that he was talking about.

This was what the Geshe had had so much to say about, so I put to Choegyal the same question as I'd put to him: if you were detached from everybody and everything, where did love for those near and dear to you come in?

'Being detached,' Choegyal replied, 'doesn't mean being indifferent. The real meaning of the word love – *agape* in the Greek – is to give without the least self-gratification. Unless you are detached from *any* kind of grasping, you cannot give selfless love. Detachment is the opposite of grasping, and it helps make sure that you are not being swallowed up by sensual pleasures.'

There was, though, one thing that it was perfectly okay to be attached to, and that was altruism, which was really – to use a Christian word he liked very much – *immaculate* love.

Meditation was also invaluable in another way. It helped to set you free from negative emotions such as anger, pride and jealousy – and from taking a misguided and unhealthy view of your life. Starting to think, for example 'I can never change' or 'If I get sick, I'm never going to get well'. After all, Jesus had said 'seek and ye shall find', and if you didn't believe that, you were definitely on the wrong road.

Choegyal was all the more impressive to me because he is humble and speaks of what he knows. He is bipolar and has been through agonising periods of depression, extreme emotional highs and lows, until he found medication – lithium – which has helped him lead an acceptably normal life. He dismisses the idea that he is in any way special – unlike his elder brother, for whom he feels both admiration and a very real reverence.

Confession, he went on, was as important in Buddhism as it was in Catholicism. If, as you meditated, you became aware that you had transgressed and had the thought that you should go to the person involved and say sorry, that was wonderful. It was atonement. I said I'd asked the Geshe whether he ever said sorry to someone he'd treated badly. There had been a silence and then he'd replied 'sometimes'. Choegyal laughed. 'Well at least he was honest', he said.

What took place in meditation amounted to an examination of conscience. That sounded rather like what a Christian might describe as listening to the Holy Spirit. 'Well,' Choegyal replied, 'we have God in us because we have the ability to love, and we have the Buddha nature because we have the ability to be enlightened.' So what did he imagine the relationship between Buddha and God to be like? He laughed again. 'I believe they exchange emails all the time', he said.

Nor did he rule out the idea of there being another voice. When Jesus was baptised, there had been a voice: 'this is my beloved son, in whom I am well pleased'. I told him that, when I was worried about whether I'd be able to do anything useful in Dharamsala, the thought had come 'Leave it to me'. I'd had no idea where the thought came from, but it didn't seem to come from me. 'Don't tell me that', said Choegyal. 'You're giving me goosebumps.'

'That other voice', he went on 'makes all the difference. Some people might say that we're mad if we talk about hearing it, but it comes, let us say, when we are in a little state of grace. I like the saying 'when you are in a state of grace, you will do the right thing' – though you can't explain where that grace comes from. That voice has to come through our thoughts, our intelligence and our saving grace'.

I thought he might be interested in what had happened to me long ago when a friend had suggested that we should sit quietly and, as he put it 'listen to God'. I'd said, 'But I don't believe in God' and he'd replied, 'That doesn't affect His position in the slightest'.

I'd expected nothing but embarrassment but, in fact, thoughts came into my mind immediately we fell quiet, thoughts I wasn't aware of ever having had before. The first, which related to the fact that I was captain of the RAF cricket team in Singapore, was 'You are a dictator on the cricket field, apologise to your team'. The second was, 'When you went up to Oxford, you became a snob. Write and apologise to your parents.'

There was a lengthy silence and then Choegyal said: 'That was a divine intervention.' 'But you don't believe that', I replied. 'Oh yes I do', he retorted with great conviction.

Then Rinchen, who thus far had said very little, came out as an oecumenical evangelist. Jesus and Buddha, she said, had both tried to bring us the same kind of light. Why did we not, together, enjoy all the marvellous things they had brought us?

Jesus was human, just like the Lord Buddha, added her husband. It was just that they were far more spiritually developed than we are. Neither of them wanted to treat us as something lower. Otherwise, why did Jesus talk about all the temptations he had had to endure?

He got up from the table and took the Spiritual Exercises of Ignatius Loyola from his bookshelf. 'He says you should meditate for seven days. That's just the same as we're supposed to do.' He roared with laughter. 'At last', he said, 'you've met two Christians!'

I said I was still puzzling about why all the Tibetans I'd met in Dharamsala seemed so cheerful and laughed so much. Here they were, huddled on this mountainside, having been exiled from a land as large as Western Europe, clinging to the remnants of their culture and civilisation, which could only serve to remind them of what they once were and had had. What did they have to laugh about?

It was true, Choegyal replied, he had often wondered whether there was any other displaced people who still had the same confidence in themselves as Tibetans did. For Tibetans, there were certainly many things that had to be dealt with seriously, but why should they get serious about them? Was that going to help?

'Despite what all our people have gone through and are still going through', said Rinchen, 'they are always very humorous. Maybe that comes from Buddhism, because Buddha always told us to take life as lightly as possible.

'One of our saints, Santi Dev, who lived in the eleventh century, advised us to do something if it helped, but not to worry about it if you couldn't. I think the ability to laugh is equal to our ability to accept things. There is a yearning in human beings to be happy. You find that in babies. When they have learned to smile, they smile all the time. To be able to really laugh, you have to have the child-like virtues'.

His Holiness, they both agreed, had helped a great deal because of his attitude to their situation. He could have been bitter and spent all his time on narrowly Tibetan issues. Instead he had taken on the needs of all humanity. Tibetans could hardly be self-centred when they had been given that sort of example.

Next morning, while I was talking with Tashi, the hotel receptionist came down in great excitement. His Holiness was coming back; he would be here quite soon.

Tashi suggested that we go up the hill to the Namygal monastery, which was next to the Palace, where His Holiness lives. On the way, we passed an ad for the Free Advanced Dental Checking Corporation, with an address which begins Near Petrol Pump, Dharamsala.

Nearby, the Tibetan Department of Health have erected a tent to help anyone who is overcome by the Dalai Lama's arrival.

We change our shoes before we go into the monastery, under a notice which suggests 'Make sure your shoes are not stolen by someone'. Inside, we are faced by a huge shrine to the bodhisattva of compassion, Avalokiteshvara – 'he has a thousand eyes and ears', says Tashi – with offerings of biscuits and honey at its feet. Next, there is a statue of Tara, who looks like a thoughtful and slightly disapproving grandmother.

Outside, there were dozens of monks wearing robes which show that many of them have attained Venerable status. 'Rather like Masters of Philosophy', explained Tashi. 'They have all done a lot of research into Buddhist texts'. Many of the monks were carrying incense sticks, and the acrid smell floated in the air.

We are told that His Holiness will arrive shortly, whereupon two young female security guards step in front of us to make sure none of us is a malefactor. They are, says Tashi, part of the Special Frontier Force. No less than 1,500 Tibetan girls had joined the force after being trained in India. One of them was his own cousin.

Just before the Dalai Lama arrived, the monks donned orange and yellow headgear and unfurled the white scarves as an earnest of their devotion to His Holiness. As his car swept up, nobody cheered, but everybody bowed. We all caught a glimpse of a smiling, observant man as he was driven into the monastery.

Tashi was much moved by the Dalai Lama's arrival and, before we parted, he had his own wisdom to impart: 'Experience is the mother of all sciences. We come from different places and by different means – some by air, some by road – but, in meditation and seeking that other voice, our destination is the same'.

I offered him a little money as a modest recompense for his help, which had been truly invaluable. He accepted it and said that he would take it immediately into the monastery as an offering from me – and for me.

Six

A House for Listening

When I discovered that the family I was thinking of visiting in Nagaland had called their home A House for Listening (Kerunyu Ki in the local, Tenyidie language), I knew I had to go there. As it turned out, listening was what was most needed in that deeply divided state in Northeast India with its plethora of tribes, clans and sub-clans, religions and races. It is, moreover, surrounded on every side not only by the India of which it is part but also by Bangladesh, China and Burma (Myanmar).

Nagaland and its one and three quarters of a million inhabitants is in the far north-east corner of India and on the Burmese border. Its capital, Kohima, is the place where British and Indian troops halted a seemingly unstoppable Japanese advance during the Second World War in an epic display of courage and endurance.

Having spent the whole of the previous night sitting on a less than comfortable chair in the airport at Calcutta, it was something of a relief to touch down at Nagaland's tiny terminal in Dimapur. I might not have felt so blithe if I'd realised that it was going to be a great deal trickier getting out of Nagaland than it was to arrive there.

For the moment, though, there was no shortage of amusement as we drove through the little town on the road towards Kohima. In Shillong, we passed a tailor's shop which announced that 'ladies have fits upstairs'. Then in Panchgani, there was a café offering 'Fried Aborigines' (aubergines?) and, finally, there was the Hairless Barbers Shop.

A House for Listening, which is perched high above the road to Kohima, turned out to be much larger than I had expected. Niketu Iralu and his wife Christine, who live there, are far from well off, living as they do without a salary of any kind. Niketu is a Naga tribal and Baptist by religion, Christine a Catholic of *very* mixed race. She describes herself as 'a little fruit salad', having English, Indian, Portuguese and Chinese blood.

Niketu, who is 80 but still has an almost child-like simplicity and openness about him, had never imagined that he and Christine would ever live in a house such as Kerunyu Ki. If they were ever able to afford a house in Nagaland, he'd always imagined that it would be 'a small is beautiful type of place', which would convey a message of living simply.

In the first ten years after he came back to Northeast India in 1995, he travelled to Dimapur in Nagaland very frequently on the overnight bus from Shillong, the capital of the neighbouring state of Meghalaya. He had friends there who were giving him and his wife a base in their home, rent-free. The bus left at four in the afternoon and arrived in Dimapur at five the next morning.

It was a long and wearisome journey of 400 kilometres on indifferent roads, but Niketu was ready to do it because he had come back home to try to heal the hatred and resentments which were poisoning Naga society.

The struggle for independence from India had been going on for decades. Many Nagas had lost their lives in that struggle, killed either by the Indian army or at the hands of their own people because of bitter disagreements about how the independence struggle should be conducted.

The divisions were so great, the hatreds so deep-seated, that, as the years went by, Niketu began to fear that they might have a civil war similar the one that occurred in Rwanda on their hands.

He started by working with the Naga Mothers' Association, who had opened a centre, Mount Gilead Home, for the rehabilitation of drug and alcohol addicts. The women who were running it admitted that they didn't know what to say to the addicts, nor even how to persuade them to listen. They could sing Gospel hymns and read Bible verses, pray with them and feed them but the addicts' only response was to bring more and more drugs and alcohol into the centre. The addicts' families were worn out, at their wits' end trying to deal with their problems. This despite the fact that Nagaland was declared a 'Dry State' by an Act of 1989. Not much has been done to implement the Act and, as a result, there is an endless flow of liquor into the officially 'dry' area.

Niketu's own family had more than its fair share of addicts. No fewer than 17 of his nephews and nieces were addicted in one way or another. Four had died, one of AIDS. Asked to run Mount Gilead, he turned to the head of the most respected rehab centre in India, Father Joe Pereira, for advice. Was it utterly foolish of him to take on the job when he'd had no training of any kind?

Pereira advised him to 'just hang in there' and promised that he would help. So Niketu decided to use the twelve-step method of Alcoholics Anonymous to persuade the addicts to accept the need for concrete and fundamental personal change – that of themselves they were powerless, that their best hope was to turn their wills and lives over to God and to begin by making a searching and fearless moral inventory of themselves.

Soon, to Niketu's surprise and delight, the centre began to produce its first, fragile recoveries. At the same time, he had become involved in a search for the healing and reconciliation of which Naga society was so deeply in need.

'The struggle for independence,' he said, 'had ended up fragmenting our society. We started to blame each other for the lack of progress. The Nagas who were fighting for freedom broke into factions and started to kill each other. In the end, we were killing more of our own people than the Indian Army'.

In his own village of Khonoma, 22 people had been murdered as a result of political differences over the way to achieve their goal. Because of the festering hatreds that these killings had left behind, the village council found it impossible to reach united decisions. In fact, they couldn't agree on anything.

They couldn't even agree about how to stop people who had begun cutting down the great trees in their beautiful virgin forests – 'our spiritual heritage', said Niketu. He became part of a committed group who tried to convince their fellow-villagers that the only answer was to set up a Khonoma Public Commission to resolve their problems. The legacy of hatred left behind by the 22 murders was clearly the main issue they had to face.

The village elders at first took the view that, if they were to bring that issue out into the open, it would only make matters worse. When they sat silently reflecting on how to move forward, however, it came to Niketu very clearly to say that, of themselves, none of them were good enough to assuage the feelings created by the killings. They were all sinners.

'Our task,' he told them, 'is to cooperate with God, because it is His task. We must cooperate with Him to find His solution'. That approach eventually won general consent and, in a mission statement, the elders told the people of the village that they couldn't get away with saying that their problems were too difficult for human beings to handle - and walk away. They had to seek God's solution which, at the time, seemed like a very tall order.

The villagers understood that kind of language perfectly well. Ninety-five per cent of Nagas are Christian, the vast majority of them Baptists. That is because a party of American missionaries heading for China towards the end of the nineteenth century had been unable to go any further and decided to try to Christianise the Nagas instead.

The result, said Niketu, was that there are literally hundreds and hundreds of churches, most of them very well supported, not to mention a superfluity of theological colleges. In his own village, there is an excellent attendance at the large Baptist church built on land donated by his father.

'They'd all been meeting together every Sunday - singing hymns and praying but not getting too close because of so many deep and unhealed feelings. They felt they couldn't talk about them even in church'.

Now, however, they responded to the idea that Christians should not only pray to God, but listen to Him and try to cooperate with Him to find out His solution to the dire situation in which they found themselves. On that basis, a process of reconciliation at last got underway in no small part because Niketu had become ever more widely trusted in Naga society. For years, he had spent his whole time, without any kind of payment, meeting members of the 17 different tribes, trying to help them with their inner anguish, offering counsel to particularly troubled individuals.

Coming, as he did, from a prominent Naga family, he could have joined the Government or sought some involvement in the politics of the State, but he didn't do either. He was not a member of any political party, not even a freedom fighter. The only thing he *was* trying to promote was the importance of the inner voice, the belief that 'we should change when we are wrong, instead of trying to justify ourselves and then praising God loudly, which we do all the time because of our shallow understanding of Christianity'.

In his view, the attitude too often was 'Christ died for our sins, so we can do anything we like', instead of trying to imitate him. 'Too many of us Christians are ready to quote bible verses and assume that then, in due course, they'll be invited to join the eternal picnic in Heaven because we are so called believers'.

Here was a man who was unlikely to tell his fellow countrymen anything less than the truth and who plainly wanted nothing for himself. That was one thing of which Nagaland was in great need.

So, when it came to the question of what kind of house he and Christine would need if they moved into Nagaland, his friends would hear nothing of his notion of a small-is-beautiful type of place.

In particular, one of the busiest and most sought after builders in the State, Ningusalie Talie, was convinced that what Niketu and Christine had to have was a place where people could meet, share their anxieties and their anger; where they could listen in quiet and try to untangle the jungle of Naga emotions and politics. Talie felt that, 'if people started to listen to one another, they might also begin to listen to God.'

Fine sentiments, but where, Niketu wondered, were they going to find the five million rupees they would need to build the sort of house that Talie had in mind? To start with, what might the builder's own services cost?

When he raised the issue, the builder's response was tart and offended. 'Did you imagine', he said, 'that, when I offered my services, I was expecting *anything* at all from you? My services will, of course, be completely free. My car, as you know, runs on water, so there won't even be any petrol expenses. No, you must be free to get on with your work. Just leave the building to me'.

Talie was as good as his word. He did not take a single rupee in the three years it took to build Kerunyu Ki, with its comfortable and spacious sitting room, bedrooms that can accommodate 17 people and its marvellous views across the valley.

That still left Niketu and Christine with five million rupees to raise. They themselves had savings of 400,000, mostly from Christine's mother. To their delight and surprise the Angamis, Niketu's own tribe, came up with two million more because they believed that Niketu had brought a new spirit to the area. The rest was given by their IoC friends from India all around the world.

Gifts also poured in from the local community. The daughter of their former host in Shillong gave a piano worth 150,000 rupees. A young man Talie had trained to become a carpenter and who now makes good-quality furniture – gave new sofas for the sitting room, while his brother provided the beds in the house. They said they were giving them because they trusted what Niketu was saying and trying to do.

When Talie spoke about the project in Khonoma, 70 or 80 people turned up at the site, offering help of various kinds. Niketu and his wife have rarely had to buy rice and people regularly bring potatoes, vegetables, chickens, and even frogs and snails. 'All that', said Niketu, 'made us feel that, by God's grace, we were doing the right thing'. In 2011, he and his family finally moved into Kerenyu Ki.

By that time, the people who had helped build the house knew just how much had been achieved through the dedication of this modest, self-effacing couple. Niketu pooh-poohs the notion that any of it is due to his own shrewdness or wisdom. 'By nature, I'm a very timid and scared little fellow. Left to myself, I'm unclear about everything. But when I ask God what He is trying to tell me, the next steps become clear.'

The first major issue that had to be dealt with, of course, was the hatred left behind by the 22 killings in his own village, Khonoma. At the Khonoma Public Commission, when it met, of which Niketu was the senior member and adviser, the village elders decided that each case would have to be tackled separately, and that a different combination of people from different clans should go to those whose families had lost someone in the murders. 'They knew exactly who should go to whom far better than me', said Niketu.

Each of the families involved were told that whoever came would come asking for forgiveness for the past. They were asked whether they were happy to receive people on that basis. In each case, the reply was that they'd been waiting for something like this for years and were ready to forgive for the sake of the village's future. 'They were all Baptists or Catholics,' said Niketu, 'so there was perhaps prepared ground'.

The most difficult case was in his own family, and the other 21 were unlikely to be solved successfully until that one had been dealt with. His uncle Phizo had been the main driving force behind the battle for independence from India and as such, had become the President of the Naga National Council. When the Indian Army started to move in, however, a younger man, Theyiechuthie Sakhrie, who was general secretary of the council, had said that they couldn't possible beat the army, and that other ways to pursue the struggle had to be found, including reaching out to the Indian people for their help and understanding.

Phizo's disagreement with Sakhrie's attitude was made worse by the fact that the young man was guilty of spreading an allegation that Phizo was seeking the assistance of Communist China. The result was that Phizo, at a meeting in a cave above Khonoma, declared that such men did not deserve to live.

Sakhrie was told by his clansmen that he was in mortal danger and should go back to his family in Shillong.

Tragically, he came back to Khonoma to see his girlfriend and was murdered by other freedom fighters who clearly interpreted Phizo's words as a death sentence.

Phizo continued to maintain, until his death, that his words had had no such import and that he was not responsible for Sakhrie's death. Niketu flew to London, where he was then living, to get him to admit his guilt, but he would not budge. The wound therefore remained unhealed, because to Sakhrie's family Phizo's outright condemnation had led to the killing of their acclaimed uncle and elder. They insisted that Phizo's moral responsibility in the tragedy could not be denied.

Sakhrie's murder was easily the most difficult of the 22 killings to be resolved. Until that had been dealt with, the other 21 were never going to be laid to rest.

Niketu began spending time with the most senior man in his own and Phizo's family, Sebi Dolie, who had been in the meeting in the cave when Phizo said that men such as Sakhrie did not deserve to live.

Sebi had welcomed the decision to try to heal all the hurts in the village but it took him time before it became clear to him what he could do about it as the elder of his own clan.

Finally, in 2010, Dolie stood up at a village meeting and declared that he wanted to put things right before he left this world. He said that he had been in the cave during the meeting, that he had heard what Phizo said, and that he had felt that, this time, Phizo had gone too far. He admitted that, ever since then, he had lived with a growing sense that he ought to make a public declaration of his convictions.

'Today,' he said to a village meeting and to Sakhrie's family in particular, 'I say that I would feel exactly as you do about

Phizo and his clan, and I ask you to forgive me and my clan. If you feel resentment about other things, please tell us, so that we may put things right properly.' Sakhrie's family were amazed and responded wholeheartedly. They had never, they said, expected to hear such a gracious apology, and they shook Dolie's hand.

Niketu took me to meet Dolie – almost blind, an old man of 88, sitting outside his modest home huddled in his robes. I congratulated him for what he had done. 'I am a very ordinary man', he replied. 'There is nothing good in me, but I do feel God has used me in a time of great division.

'I'm very clear that, despite my unworthiness, God has kept me alive to do something for His plan. When we were told, 'don't think of where others have been wrong, only where you have been wrong', I decided to go to the church and be silent. In that moment, I gave my life to God completely.

'I thought I would hear something from Heaven, but although I did not hear anything, I felt that God was entering me. Since I spoke up at the meeting, I have lived with inner peace, feeling that I have been used by God. I, and all of us, had to go down to our very deepest roots and, because of facing what was wrong, we have been washed clean. Nobody brings those things up any more. Even drunkards in their worst moments have never referred to those killings again.' All the other 21 cases were resolved, equally happily. Khonoma is no longer in thrall to the past.

In the years that followed, more and more people asked to come and spend time at Kerunyu Ki. Villagers from all over Nagaland chose it as a place where they could thrash out issues that were troubling them. Ten, fifteen, thirty people would sit around in the meeting room and start to say all that was on their hearts.

'We'll often ask people to be quiet', said Niketu, 'tell them that this is a house of listening where we listen both to one another and also to what is going on in our own hearts, souls and consciences because God may want to speak to us. Our people are only too used to praying, but many of them find it intriguing to be asked to listen'.

Some of the leaders of the Bodo people, the most widely spread group in the nearby Assam valley, have also found their way to Kerunyu Ki. Like the Nagas they were killing each other; their society, too, was riven by violence and corruption. Niketu and Christine spoke at a workshop in the Catholic Retreat Centre in Shillong and shared their own experience of listening to the inner voice.

As a result, 17 leaders of the all-Bodos came to a two-day workshop at Kerunyu Ki. The presidents and general secretaries of the various districts were among them. Niketu suggested a time of listening and, afterwards, the Bodos began to speak of all they had been through. One of the presidents said he had suffered injuries while trying to stop his father beating his mother during his frequent bouts of drunkenness.

Others spoke of their anxieties for their children, the despair and emptiness of their lives. Many were intrigued by the idea that God might have something to say to them. They began to wonder if listening and what came to them in silence might be a new way to find an answer to the things that made them despair – and might even redirect their lives. 'They came alive again during those times', said Niketu. 'It gave them a new sense of adventure.'

Months after they had gone back home, one of the Bodos telephoned in great distress and told Niketu that, although he had recently got married, he had since become too fond of a woman he worked with. He'd been honest with his wife about it and, although she had found it very difficult, she had forgiven him. Could he, the Bodo asked, bring her to Kerunyu Ki?

Of course, replied Niketu, and added that the man was just like him. He had, he confessed, exactly the same temptations but that, when he thought of the needs of Naga society, it helped him to hold on to what he knew was right. Otherwise he too would be at the mercy of his flesh.

One of Niketu's strengths, as it seems to me, is that he doesn't try to appear too wise or too good, to set himself above those he is trying to help, to convey a sense that he knows all the answers. When he was a student in Madras, he had an experience of what he felt was the other voice and longs to help others share that experience.

When he went to Madras University in 1955 to study English literature, he was the first of his tribe to go there. He was, he says, the shyest and most backward in his class. He'd read nothing much more than *Reader's Digest* and the Bible, whereas all the others had read Shakespeare, Milton and Dickens. He knew he'd have to do a paper on Anglo-Saxon and it gave him nightmares.

Aware that, back home, his people were fighting the Indian Army, he wondered how Nagaland could possibly survive in the world. Having been an appendage of the British Empire, he like his people didn't want it to become an appendage of India. He felt deeply insecure and profoundly bitter.

It was then that he met a bunch of people from IoC who said that, if we wanted things to change, it had to start with ourselves. They also talked about listening in silence to anything God might have to say to us.

'Baptists,' said Niketu, 'know more than anybody else about prayer. We used to pray very loudly and indicate to God exactly what we thought should happen. I wondered if there might be something in the idea of giving God the chance to speak'.

When the people in the group suggested that they might try the idea and sit in silence together, it turned out to be a pivotal moment in his life. 'They gave us all bits of paper on which to write down any thoughts we had. At first I didn't get anything and I thought "I'm not learning anything here".'

'Then, very clearly it came to me: 'You are a very selfish man, you are jealous of many people in Nagaland and you love nobody.' When the time of listening came to an end, I thought that more would have been revealed to me if it had been longer – though what had come was quite enough! Whether it was a voice or not, it was very clear – a version of the experience of Hagar in the Book of Genesis. Hagar is said to have been visited twice by angels – could that, he wondered, be a Biblical version of interior locutions?

When the group began to share their thoughts with each other, and asked Niketu what he had written down, he replied that it was nothing important and that he didn't want to waste their time. He'd always said and thought that he wasn't very important and felt like a very frightened little boy in a great big world.

One of the group pressed him to say what he'd thought. When he told the group what had come to him with such clarity, the man leading the meeting congratulated him on his courage and honesty and added that, if he went on listening to those thoughts and obeying them, he would be able to help his people. It turned out to be a rather prophetic remark.

Niketu decided to go on with the experiment of giving God the chance to speak to him and, when asked by one of his new friends, to be specific about his selfishness, he told the story of finding that the light bulb in his room was too weak and switching it with the one from the bathroom, which was far stronger. He didn't worry about what happened to the other people who used the bathroom. In one of his times of listening, he saw that that was selfish and changed the bulbs back again – but at night, when no one could see him.

In his next time of listening, he thought that that was still not good enough and that he ought to tell the hotel superintendent, who happened to be an Anglican priest.

He didn't actually go to see him for quite a while, assuming that the priest would think 'this Naga boy, he really is pathetic'. But when he knocked on the superintendent's door, said he was sorry and asked for forgiveness, the superintendent not only thanked him but said 'Keep it up', and gave him the firmest of handshakes.

Niketu's father, Sevilie, had been put in jail simply because he was the brother-in-law of the freedom fighter Phizo. Sevilie was one of the first Nagas to become a doctor and had helped the British during the war with free medical treatment and as a supplier of funds for espionage raids against the Japanese.

Niketu decided to write to him and admit that the 'beautiful' (but entirely fictional) accounts of how he was spending his money were just a pack of lies. He had told his father that he had spent it buying books for the English Literature course, whereas in fact he'd been buying books about sex.

His father's reply was completely unexpected. 'My dear son,' he wrote, 'when people are honest in that way, it must be God.' Then he added, 'I know how you children [there were 12 of them] feel about the way I treat your mother. I say wounding things to her because she has no idea how to manage money. I promise to treat her differently when I come out.' And, said Niketu, he did.

Niketu's father wanted him to try to win a place in the Indian mandarinate, the Administrative Service. Instead, he chose to spend his life working, without salary, with his IoC friends. In time, his father came to respect that choice.

He watched Niketu trying to reconcile warring groups of Nagas and trying to persuade their people to overcome their differences and work together for an honourable and workable settlement with India. Niketu has spoken at hundreds of meetings, large and small, on several occasions to as many as 10,000 of his people.

He describes himself as a secessionist, who would like India to treat Nagaland as one of its neighbours. That, however, he admits, would require the Nagas to start working hard to solve their own problems.

'Unless we stop being lazy and selfish', he says, 'and just go on blaming India, it is going to destroy us. So much of our money is given to us by Delhi and, as a result we have become easy-going and, too often, drunk'. Because he has made it clear that he holds these views, Niketu has been accused by other Nagas of being a tool of Indian Intelligence.

The whole system, he told me, is riddled with corruption. The Indian government supplied money for cement, rice, corrugated iron sheets, all kinds of things, and there were Indian contractors and suppliers who skimmed the money. 'These suppliers get to know the Indian bureaucrats, and they work out deals with the result that a lot of things never arrive in Nagaland'.

His battle goes on. On the day after I was due to depart, he was flying to Chiang Mai in Thailand to a meeting aimed at trying to find unity between the seven different Naga factions. Interestingly, it was Niketu's Quaker friends in London, and not the Nagas, who insisted that he must be there. He went, as ever, hoping for a miracle.

The day before I was due to fly out of Nagaland, on my way to Amman in Jordan, there came news of truly horrific events in Dimapur. A woman had been raped, the man thought to be guilty, a Bangladeshi, had been arrested but then dragged out of prison and slaughtered by a frenzied mob. They were said to number as many as 30,000.

Given that the Bangladeshi was a Muslim, the Muslims in the area had turned out in force, and there was a real risk of inter-faith violence. The result was that anyone using the road, through Dimapur, might well be in serious danger. I was strongly advised by the local police not to travel until peace had been restored.

In the light of these dreadful developments, my own travel arrangements were of piddling importance, but the fact was that I somehow had to find a way out of Nagaland the very next morning. My hosts tried their hardest to find a way of getting me to the airport in Jorhat safely. They asked the police superintendent for an escort, but were told that he was going to need all his men just to keep the peace.

It looked hopeless. Then, astonishingly, a young woman who as staying with us in Kerunyu Ki remarked that her father happened to be a superintendent of the state helicopter service. She wondered whether there might be a chance that he could help me.

She telephoned him and discovered that, the very next morning, a helicopter had already been arranged to take an elderly lady who had had a stroke to the hospital at Guwarhati in Assam. Was there any way, she asked, that he might be able to find a seat for me? It seemed like a very long shot, but it was my last hope.

There were then protracted negotiations on the telephone about whether the helicopter could accommodate my luggage as well as me. At one point, the superintendent said I'd have to leave it behind if he found me a seat. Then he asked how large my biggest suitcase was. Would it be too large? It was going to be a tight squeeze in any case. He wasn't sure he could authorise it, but his daughter was very persistent and persuasive.

Finally, to my immense relief, he agreed to let me have a ticket. So, next day, Niketu drove me to the helicopter pad in Kohima. There, I waited for a nail-biting hour and a half before, at last, the helicopter flew into sight. The old lady and three of her relatives were safely stowed aboard – and I was given the last seat. No sigh of relief and gratitude has ever been more heartfelt.

As the philosopher Alain de Botton says: 'To feel grateful is to allow oneself to sense how much one is at the mercy of events. It is to accept that there may come a point when our extraordinary plans for ourselves have run aground.' Until the possibility of the helicopter surfaced, mine most certainly had.

Seven

The Humble American

When I climbed aboard that helicopter, I fondly imagined that my travelling trials were over. Not quite. We were late into Dubai – with its vast, unforgiving airport – and although, by far exceeding my normal pace, I managed to make the starting gate in time, the despatcher refused to allow me aboard.

I pointed out that I had a ticket and a boarding pass but, she insisted, I was too late to be allowed onto the plane. Why, for goodness sake? Because, she explained, my luggage would not have made the transition as quickly as I had. She did not, it seemed, want me to arrive in Amman luggage-less – and she was quite adamant about it.

Never mind what I, the passenger, wanted. Was it, I wondered, because she had had it drummed into her that the cost of delivering late luggage was going to affect the airline's profits? I could not think of any other reason for holding me up.

There was far more at stake than she realised. This was a crisis only marginally less serious than the affair in Nagaland. It was not just a question of me having to wait for the next flight to Jordan, with all the irritating changes in arrangements which would then be necessary.

What was much, much worse was that I was being met in Amman by my Muslim hosts – and if I wasn't on the expected flight, it might ruin the whole trip to Amman, because I wouldn't have any way of getting in touch with them. I had no telephone number for them and no email address, I didn't even know the surname of the man who was to be my host. How would I ever find him in a city to which I had never been before?

I didn't know how to get across to this implacable despatcher the magnitude of the crisis which faced me. I tried, several times, but she simply shook her head. I fancy that, at first, she thought I was just trying it on. Then, thank heaven, she noticed the extent of my distress – controlled frenzy would be a more accurate description – and she began a long series of telephone calls to an invisible superior, asking if she could let me aboard.

This went on for five, ten minutes. Utterly nerve-wracking. Was the plane, I wondered, going to depart before she got an answer? Were the airline's profits an immovable sticking point? Finally, reluctantly, she waved me up the gangway. Once there, I received immediate compensation for my anguish: I had been upgraded to business class.

Even better, when we arrived in Amman, there was Anas, my host, smiling broadly, waiting to sweep me off into the city. He is English, tall and slim, with a gingery beard and all the cheerfulness of someone who has found a satisfying faith in Islam. I had first met him in Damascus a dozen or so years before when I was working for the *Daily Telegraph*.

He and his wife Naielah are part of a community of a hundred or so Sufi families who look up to Sheikh Nuh Keller, an American who has lived in the Middle East for more than 30 years, as their spiritual guide and master. They include businessmen such as Anas, at least one doctor, students doing doctorates and directors of language schools.

To be a Sufi sheikh who is permitted to teach, you have to have been given a licence – *ijaza* - by a sheikh who is authorised to grant them. Nuh had been given his licence by a sheikh in Damascus called Abd al-Rahman al-Shaghouri. I was glad the sheikh I'd come to meet was called something altogether shorter and sweeter.

Nuh and his followers around the world belong to the Shadhili sect of sufism which, Anas tells me, follows a path which focusses on love and 'melting one's heart' in gratitude to God, which sounds irreproachable. Like the other major sufi sects, they also aim at direct communion with God and spend a good deal of time in introspection.

At the apartment block where Anas lives, two women in full burkas – completely covered save for their eyes – greeted me. No names were exchanged since, as I discovered, it is thought improper for a man to address a woman, other than his wife, by her own name. Nonetheless and despite the restrictions of their dress, they immediately made me feel welcome. All I could see was their smiling eyes, but they exuded genuine warmth and a sense, without using words, that they were glad that I was to be their guest.

Anas owns two apartments, no doubt the fruit of the small but successful company he runs which sells the sort of clothes devout Muslims like to wear. I was to stay in the apartment just across the passage from the one where he and his wife live.

On the door of my flat were the words 'Dignity, Reverence, Serenity, Love and High Aspiration'. That sounded like a pretty tall order, but at least you knew what was expected of you – and, more to the point, of the Sheikh's followers. Before we went in, Anas instructed me in the footwear etiquette I was required to observe.

Outdoor shoes were to be taken off, left outside and replaced by unsullied indoor slippers. Then, when I wanted to use the bathroom, these slippers were to be replaced by a different pair, a little like Crocs and suitable for a wet environment.

I noticed, en passant, that there was no mirror of any kind in the bathroom. Was this, I wondered, a deterrent to vanity or did it have something to do with the fact that all male Sufis have beards? In any case, it seemed odd. When it came to shaving, I had to use a tiny mirror taken from the lounge and perch it on a low radiator in the bathroom. It was the first time I had ever shaved kneeling down.

There were other, more significant, oddities still to come. Naielah, Anas's Trinidad-born wife, was my hostess for a week, yet I never once saw her in her own home, still less talked to her.

She cooked some delightful meals for Anas and myself, but never once appeared in the dining room. She would call to her husband from the kitchen when the food was ready, and he would go and bring it in.

I noticed that he made quite sure that the double doors between the two rooms were always fully closed as he went out and came in, so that I would not be able to catch even the merest glimpse of his wife. Similarly, when I left at the end of the meal, he always made sure that the coast was clear, that his wife was not doing something in the hall where I might encounter her. For me, at that stage, Naielah remained just a disembodied voice.

'Our rules for social intercourse between the sexes are really very strict', said Anas. 'They make quite sure that there is no chance of even the least extra-marital hanky-panky. My own parents are divorced and so I've seen for myself what devastation that has wrought in our family'.

If wives showed themselves to men to whom they were not married, who knew where it might lead? He preferred to play it safe. He had seen the cost of the western way.

'Given that there are a lot of 20- and 30-year-olds in our community,' agreed Dr Syed Rehan, who has been with the Sheikh for 16 years, 'Nuh has told us that we should keep a distance between the sexes. At our supper parties, for example, the women eat separately from the men. The men collect the dishes and serve it to the men, and the women serve themselves.

'Contact between the sexes is based on need. Even then, if you talk to a woman, you tend to do so with your face turned away. I have female patients within the community and see women all the time, but it is strictly business, never flirty'.

I wondered whether the sufi women didn't find it boring to be quite unable to lead a normal life. Not at all, replied Anas, the women were entirely happy with a life that didn't include men. They found social intercourse with their sisters entirely satisfying. I didn't have the chance to ask the sisters whether they agreed.

Anas was at some pains to make sure that I realised there was no notion of asceticism in their version of Islam. They were not monks sitting on top of hills. They weren't expected to deny the needs of the body – food and sex – though these were not an end in themselves, but a means of coming closer to God.

Wives took delight in their husbands, husbands took delight in their wives. None of the major varieties of sufism required the denial of legitimate sexual desires.

That same evening, I went for the first time to one of the Sheikh's teachings. It took place in a large, carpeted hall empty of furniture and lit by a large, simple candelabra. Groups of men, and they were, of course, all men, were reading or chatting quietly along the walls. They were mostly bearded and youngish. Several smiled at me in welcome. I did not feel like an intruder, even a stranger. The women were in a glass-fronted gallery above the hall.

When Nuh arrived, his disciples knelt or squatted at his feet at the far end of the hall. He is a man in his fifties, fresh-faced and lean, with a light greyish beard. He was dressed, unostentatiously, in a long robe, with a simple white hat and a scarf around his neck.

He began by praying quietly and ardently, eyes closed, hands open and out-stretched. When he began the teaching, his voice was so low that he was occasionally inaudible, to me at least. His whole manner was the very opposite of declamatory, closer to a murmur than a rallying-cry. And there was lightness, too, and humour, as the teaching went on.

Nonetheless, on that first evening and on subsequent ones, there was also a passionate bite in what he had to say. He described the love of this world and its values, the desire to have prestige in its eyes, as nothing more than 'filth'. It was part of that filth to have a yearning to be popular, to long to be thought well of by others.

Hellfire, he declared, was what awaited those who lauded their supremacy over others. In doing that, they were simply aping the tyrants and oppressors – and, in due course, would suffer the same fate as those tyrants. Lowliness was the way to happiness. As for those who felt admiration for themselves, who adopted a high tone, pushed others down, that was the path of death.

We should all, he said, run towards Allah. Sin grated on the conscience, we hated other people to know about the pathetic and disgusting things we did which chafed upon our minds. We should never be vulgar or obscene, crude or coarse – or, for that matter, grasping and stingy. Graciousness, kindness, generosity, that was the road to take. It was an entirely one-way process. The sheikh spoke and his followers listened in rapt silence. There were no questions.

There was something oddly compelling about Nuh. The monotone in which he spoke, the fact that he never raised his voice, had something to do with it. It was an odd tone in which to propound old-time, full-bore religion at its most demanding and uncompromising. It became all the more compelling when, as I discovered later, Nuh did not exempt himself from the strictures which he pressed upon his disciples.

Then it was time to stagger up the steep hill to the mosque, where hundreds of men were arriving for the last prayer of the day. There was nothing formal about their dress. Again, everyone was both friendly and considerate. One man asked me whether I was being taken care of. Young children came to shake my hand. It was the exact opposite of the mental attitudes of those who belong to Islamic State. With the Sufis of Amman, there is no hostility to anyone, no matter where they come from. The fact that the sheikh is American says it all.

On the wall of the mosque's small and simple hall were a list of pairs of red numbers. In a Christian church, they would be the numbers of the hymns. Here, they indicate the times of day when the various prayers should be said. The first prayer of the day, they indicated, should take place between 4.35 and 5.51 am in the cold, grey half-light before the dawn – a spread which, I suppose, is intended to give believers at least a modicum of choice.

There is certainly nothing casual about the way the sufis go about prayer. They stand shoulder to shoulder in prescribed ranks, literally toeing the same line. They obey the instructions of the imam instantly – stand, crouch, squat, abase themselves as he commands. This is synchronised worship, total unison for 15 or 20 minutes of physically vigorous prayer. It has something of the precision of a military parade; though the prayers which the faithful offer in silence are highly individual and have nothing to do with the imam. Sheikh Nuh, I noticed, had now become simply one of the congregation.

This is just a part of the rigorous lifestyle that he requires of his disciples. Mysticism is often thought of as being rather unspecific but vaguely connected to spirituality, a way of lifting us out of the mundane and into a more enlightened state of being. It is apt to be woolly, ill-defined, soft edged. Well, there is nothing woolly or soft-edged about Sheikh

Nuh's version of mysticism. On the contrary, it is extremely hard-edged. 'You could,' he told me, 'call it hard-style sufism'.

There is, of course, regular prayer, five times every day, usually in the mosque. That, however, is just the framework of devotion. Nuh also believes that there has to be an ethical basis to religious mysticism and, to that end, sets his followers a whole series of exercises that require them to make a scrupulous moral scrutiny of the way they are living.

He expects them to be constantly vigilant. This is called *muraqaba*.

The first of the seven exercises he sets his followers is known among them as the 40-grand. It comes in two parts. The first part is that, for 40 consecutive days, they must perform all the obligatory prayers. Miss one and, rather like a game of snakes and ladders, they have to go back to the beginning again.

The second part of the test is that, for the same 40 days, they must not fall into any extreme expressions of anger – berating their wife or one of their colleagues, slamming doors and so on. If they explode, lose control of themselves just once, it is back to day one again.

'The second exercise,' as Anas explained, 'is that for ten consecutive days, you must be entirely free from sins of the tongue. That includes lying, back-biting, being critical of someone behind their backs – 'he talks too much', for example, or 'he's too fat' – and saying anything which is intended to show what a splendid person you are – 'I prayed for 45 minutes today', that kind of thing.

'All of that is *haram*, forbidden. And you are also expected to refrain from speaking about things when there is no need to do so – telling about how corrupt our society has become, for example'.

'The third exercise,' said Anik Abdullah, who is the director of a language school, 'is all about complaining and moaning, particularly to people who can't do anything about the situation. If your children are being bullied, of course, it is right to complain to the superintendent of the school, but if you are just complaining about your neighbour or the way life is treating you, you shouldn't. In those cases, the only person who can do anything about it is God, so do your complaining to Him – but, at the same time, remember to praise Him for all the things which are going well'.

And on it goes. 'Another exercise,' Abdullah went on, 'is to make sure that you've paid off *all* your debts. Even if it has just involved stealing candy from a grocery store when you were a child, some kind of restitution has to be made. You could do that anonymously, but you must make amends.'

The final exercise, said Anas, was one of the hardest. It involved very deep, honest introspection as to your feelings about other people – those you disliked and why you disliked them – and then somehow getting rid of those bad feelings and making sure you didn't hold a grudge against anyone. It was *extremely* difficult.

As if all that were not enough, the sheikh then asks his disciples to go through the exercises for a second time, not cutting themselves any slack as they might have done the first time round, but this time 'without wearing kid gloves', as Abdullah put it.

To Nuh, indeed, it is an endless process. One of his disciples once told him that he was just starting on the last exercise. Nuh replied that it wasn't the last exercise, just the beginning.

'Through those seven stages,' Nuh said, 'we move from the outward to the inward human being. It requires a great deal of reflection and resolve. You're trying to dig out the poisonous chemicals and put in better soil. You don't build a beautiful garden on a chemical waste dump!

'But when souls, as I've learned from experience, fix their firm resolve to leave all their sins behind, they can then roam freely in the spiritual world and return with exquisite pearls of wisdom'.

If one of the disciples gets into difficulty of some kind, the sheikh is readily available to help. 'When you lapse,' said Abdullah, 'you can share the problem with Nuh and get advice about how to overcome it. I can walk with him every single day or book a private meeting on a Friday. He's always accessible.'

At the end of every day, before they take to their beds, the disciples are also expected, as Anas puts it, 'to hold the ego to account for any contraventions of *muraqaba*,' to look back critically at the way they have behaved that day. This is called *muhasaba*, which is a way of keeping short accounts with God. They are then expected to repent and pray the prayer of forgiveness. 'One weeps', said Anas, 'or at least tries to summon up tears'.

The sheikh clearly applies the same rigorous standards to himself: 'For me, continual repentance is the expectation, that is the fuel of the spiritual path. The lower you humble yourself to the divine, the higher the soul can rise. We are infinitely flawed. You have to realise just how pathetic you are. If you don't, then you are not a sufi.'

97

The main point of all this rigour, of course, is to bring the sufi closer to God. 'We do it,' said Abdullah, 'to make ourselves better receivers of God's communication with us to take away the obstacles between Allah and ourselves'.

In what form, then, do these communications arrive? Sufis say they are very doubtful about hearing an actual voice. For them, they argue, it is altogether too anthropomorphic a concept, appearing to express contact with a God who has human characteristics.

Yet they have the notion of *hatif*, the Arabic word for telephone, but which also means 'the caller', the voice – as it were – of someone speaking to you. They use the phrase 'answering the caller', in other words responding to the disembodied voice – and clearly regard it as one way in which Allah communicates with the faithful.

'In most cases', said Um Sahl, Sheikh Nuh's wife, who was born in Albania but is now a New Zealander, 'the people who receive a *hatif* feel that it has brought them closer to Allah'.

In the minds of Nuh's disciples, there is no doubt that the rigour of these seven exercises help them to become aware of that other voice. That's when the other conversation starts to take place within you, said Anas. I get what I call little notes from God all the time as I go through life, kindnesses which we are apt to call coincidences, though they happen very often'.

Then there are, of course, the *warids* – or *khatirs* as they are sometimes known – the thoughts and inclinations which come into their minds 'from elsewhere', as one disciple put it.

Sufis are extremely reluctant to share their own spiritual experiences. They do not 'witness' in the Christian sense. They feel that, in doing so, they are putting themselves on a spiritual pedestal, being boastful about what Allah has given them.

One, however, decided to break the general rule providing he remained anonymous. 'I was struggling with a sin which I couldn't get rid of for many years', he said. 'Then I went to a spiritual gathering called a *hadra* and towards the end, I had a very intense experience. I had a communication, a feeling which took over my whole body and essence. It told me that, providing I did not go back to the sin, God had completely forgiven me. I did feel completely free.'

According to Sheikh Ali, a distinguished scholar, who has been teaching Sheikh Nuh and his wife for ten years, the Koran – like the Bible – is full of stories of God speaking to people. 'Joseph, when he was down the well, received a message from an angel or directly from God, telling him not to worry or panic. The mother of Moses, when Pharaoh started killing babies, was told that, if she was worried, she should put him into a basket beside the stream. Then she was told that she shouldn't be either scared or sad, because Allah would return Moses to her and that He intended to make her son one of His messengers.

'Again, there is the story of the mother of Mary, Jesus's mother, who prayed to God when she was pregnant with Mary, saying that she wanted a boy and promising that he would be completely devoted to Allah in the mosque. Well, the baby turned out to be a girl who became Jesus' mother, so God gave Mary something better than she had asked for. In my mind, there really is no doubt that God speaks to people'.

For his part, Sheikh Nuh believes that there are four levels of thought. The first is the normal chitter-chatter which goes on in our head all the time. Then there are devilish thoughts, which impel us to do evil things. The third, the work of angels, incline us to do unselfish things for which we will receive no return. The fourth level is thoughts sent by God. 'They are thoughts which push me to take a certain course of action', he said. 'The notion of an actual voice I regard with suspicion – the speaking mind is not the apex of human intelligence according to sufi thought, we're much keener on intuition or instinct. But I'm very happy with the idea of impulses which don't come from our normal thought processes'.

When Sufis were faced with alternatives on important issues, he went on, they prayed the *istikhara* prayer. That asked God to open their hearts to discern what was the best of the alternatives before them, and to bring that alternative to come to pass.

In his own home, the sheikh conveys the same aura of reflective simplicity and humility as he did when teaching. He had been brought up, he told me, in the wheat and cattle country of Washington State. His mother was a nurse, his father a pharmacist. That was why he was apt to use medical metaphors.

He now has several thousand disciples around the world and, needless to say, a website Unto the One.

The shadhili way of sufism, to which he had given his life, was simply a way of giving thanks to Allah for all He has given us. That was the 'fastest way to untie the egotistical knot'. After all, if you couldn't take credit for anything because you'd been given your health and intelligence by someone else, there was nothing on which you could pride yourself. So, instead of me-ism, it was a thank you.

This is the very opposite of the horrors which Islamic State have been perpetrating, in the name of Islam, just a few hundred miles from where we were talking. Those people, said Nuh, all subscribed to the sect of Wahhabism, founded in the eighteenth century by Mohammed ibn Abdul Wahab, a sect which was narrow and intolerant to the last degree. Islamic State was 100 per cent Wahhabi.

Sufism and Wahhabism, he went on, were the two opposing camps fighting for the hearts and souls of Muslims. At the moment, he had to admit, there was no doubt that the Wahhabis had the upper hand. They were, quite literally, calling the shots.

What had happened was that the Saudis – where Wahhabism was the controlling form of Islam – had thrown a great deal of money at buying all the people they could, recruiting students from all over the world to brain-wash them with Wahhabi ideas. The result was that Wahhabism had become the default setting for many otherwise harmless Muslims, and the default setting in many mosques.

Their beliefs were utterly opposed to those of traditional Islam. For many centuries, it had been an extremely tolerant religion – under the Ottoman Empire, for example, Christians and Jews had had their own courts – and sufism was entirely in favour of that tolerant view. The trouble was, it had no money, but at least it formed islands, oases of those who understood the true nature of Islam.

'There are students from 90 countries in Saudi Arabia at the moment', said Um Sahl, his wife. 'They are given the whole thing for free. The Saudis pay for their air tickets, they give them a monthly salary and promise that they will learn Arabic in a sacred city such as Medina. For the last 30 years, thousands of students have been going there getting their heads filled with this rubbish.

'It's a puritanical movement which wants to take Islam back into the past. No Islamic scholar of any merit would regard the motor car as an innovation, but the Wahhabis say that the Prophet rode on a camel, so therefore you must not drive a car. Even prayer beads, which I use when I pray, are regarded as a reprehensible innovation.

'Ours is a religion of mercy, but let these people grab the steering wheel and what will people all over the world think of Islam? They are preventing a religion of goodness and mercy coming into people's lives'. Like her husband, she feels the deepest frustration and sadness that the Wahhabis of Islamic State are fatally besmirching the image of Islam all over the world.

One evening, at the mosque, I met Drilon Gashi, a Kosovan who is doing a Masters in Islamic Studies. He had previously been a student in Saudi Arabia – drawn there, as he admitted, by Saudi money – but had left when he could stand it no longer.

'The atmosphere there was that you had to toe the line', he said. 'If you had ventured a different opinion, you would have been kicked out of the university and your grant stopped. IS is a direct product of that system, whereas here there is toleration and openness. Some of the Wahhabi scholars actually say that, if you stop at traffic lights, you are following a model laid down in the West and not God's law.

'They would take the view that I am now no longer a Muslim and that it would be quite permissible to kill me. So far as they are concerned, it is perfectly okay to kill Muslims who are outside their fold.'

It was something of a relief when my hosts offered me a trip to the Dead Sea, with historical sights including an old Roman port thrown in. What a treat, I thought! Um Sahl would go with me, along with one of her female colleagues – who turned out to be Anas's wife - and Anas himself made up the party. I visualised a day off, taking it easy in the sunshine after five weeks of conversations in India and Jordan. I was in for a surprise.

We had scarcely started when Um Sahl started bombarding me up with a cannonade of searching questions. What, she wanted to know, was I trying to do with this book? What was my perspective? Did I yearn for God? The tone was cool and not unduly friendly. I realised that back-seat interrogators could be as annoying as back-seat drivers.

She also wanted to make sure that I knew that the Koran was an unadulterated communication from God, and that there were also 30,000 *hadiths* – sayings of the Prophet – which had been totally and beyond question authenticated.

The Koran was a revelation of the Prophet given to him over the course of 23 years and, although he was illiterate, it was written in the most beautiful Arabic which even the simplest Arab could understand.

One of its focuses was the refining of the heart and soul. There was a word – ubudiyya – which meant slavehood and another – isal – which meant submission to God in love and sincerity and dread. I knew Um Sahl was utterly genuine and meant well, but it did sound thoroughly unattractive. When she said that she had no intention of proselytising, I could forbear no longer. 'You could have fooled me', I burst out.

That did not stop Um Sahl's passionate exposition. For her, she went on, the soul was the essence of the human being, and it had several levels.

The first, *Nafs*, was the equivalent of the ego, the lower self. It was the domain of the Devil. The second level, *Aql*, was that of the intellect, the thinking soul which was able to entertain the possibility that God existed. The third level was *Qalb*, the heart, where we had begun to turn to spiritual things. The fourth, *ruh* or spirit, was where we engaged in the remembrance of God and began to be aware of His majesty. Ruhr-al-quds means Sacred Spirit.

The soul's fifth and final level was *sirr*, which literally meant the secret, and that was when the majesty of God finally dawned in our hearts and our focus on self dwindled away.

Then, quite suddenly, she switched from exposition to persuasion and began to try to convince me that I should become a Muslim. It was, she said, 'the yearning of her heart' that I should convert. That was her heartfelt wish 'from my heart to yours'.

Her ardour and her genuineness were touching, if slightly embarrassing. She wanted, she went on, to make the process easy for me. If I thought I couldn't do it all at once, that didn't stop me becoming a Muslim. Even if I didn't practise, I could still become a Muslim in *belief*, and that was what mattered.

All I had to do to enter into the covenant of the Prophet was to declare that I believed in Allah and his Prophet. Of course if I could practice as well, there would be many more blessings.

When I was alone, in quiet, I should implore God to tell me what He wanted of me and then assure Him that I meant to obey. 'You are only required to be sincere,' said Umm Sahl, and you'll get lifted up by helicopter!'

Perhaps to give me a further nudge in the right direction, she pointed out the things in Christianity which Muslims couldn't believe. For example, they didn't believe that Jesus had been crucified, it was someone else. At the end of time, Jesus would return and go to Damascus.

Then, so far as Muslims were concerned, the whole idea of the Trinity, God in three persons – which, incidentally, hadn't been mentioned at all until the 130s AD – was nothing more than polytheism. Putting a man-God in the place where only Allah should be.

Since I believe wholeheartedly in the Trinity, that did not make her offering any more attractive. Touched as I was, I managed to sidestep the invitation. And, after that, we had a delightful day, and Umm Sahl was the most thoughtful of hostesses.

This wasn't the only time when one of Sheikh Nuh's Sufis tried to engage me in a spot of theological back and forth. At the end of our conversation, Drilon the Kosovan came up with a quotation from St Mark's Gospel where Jesus says that heaven and earth would pass away, but that neither men nor angels nor even the Son knew the hour or the day when that would take place. Only God the Father knew that.

How, Drilon wanted to know, could Jesus possibly be God if He didn't know. Because God surely knew everything? How could I believe in a religion which was not rationally acceptable?

There were, he went on, two pieces of land and a man was given money to work on one but, instead, went to work on the other. I didn't quite understand what he was telling me, but I replied – perhaps rather lamely – that he'd just have to realise that I was a hopeless case who tried to obey the God who owned both pieces of land.

Then one of Sheikh Ali's friends told me, over a cup of coffee, that he'd had a dream about me that very afternoon. In the dream, I had been prostrating myself and holding out my hand with one finger pointing forward. That, he said, was a sign that I had accepted the Oneness of God.

But then, in the dream, there was a woman sitting to the right. She was not covered, she was not a Muslim. She got up to see if I was still alive, but by then I had then sat up.

He had, Sheikh Ali's friend went on, looked up the meaning of the dream. The woman was a representation of worldliness – dunya – but he had seen from my actions that I was moving towards God because prostration was a sign of slavehood. He didn't know whether the dream meant that I would or should become a Muslim.

Then Sheikh Ali and I had a debate about the Trinity and the importance of correct belief. But did correct belief, I asked, inevitably produce good behaviour? After all, the followers of Islamic State no doubt all believed in the Oneness of God, yet still committed unspeakably barbarous acts. So was actual behaviour not the key test?

The Sheikh did not dispute that behaviour was crucial – and then his anger boiled over. What Islamic State were doing was appalling. 'Our religion', he said, 'is a religion of love and affability but what would you think if you watched the TV news?' I couldn't help but feel for him.

Whatever was happening further to the north, Sheikh Nuh and his band of disciples are flourishing and deserve to do so. They are a deeply impressive community. They are planning to build a new and larger mosque and they will call it *Al Bushra*, which means great glad tidings.

Eight

College of the Inner Voice

It could only happen in India. Each year, 25 of the country's most senior civil servants and 300 of its industrial chief executives come to Asia Plateau, IoC's conference centre at Panchgani, 4,000 feet up in the beautiful Sahyadri mountains of Maharashtra, 285 miles south-east of Mumbai.

And what do they go there for? A seminar on cost benefit analysis, perhaps, or a symposium on government-business relations? Nothing of the kind. They go, believe it or not, to learn about the Inner Voice or Antaratma – the Hindi word for conscience or soul – and how listening to it can give them truly fulfilling and creative lives.

The thought of senior Western bureaucrats and businessmen doing any such thing would beggar belief, but that is what Panchgani is about – and more and more of their Indian counterparts are choosing to go there.

It is the same experience for all the 2,000-plus people who arrive at the centre each year – 600 middle managers, 200 teachers and their families, 400 local government executives and 700 students from all over the world. For each of them, their time in Asia Plateau will be about quiet times and the

Inner Voice 'speaking' in that silence which can transform their lives.

When they arrive, they are all – mandarins and students alike – given the same little yellow notebook, where they are told to write down whatever they receive from the Inner Voice. The little book is perfectly straightforward about the process they are expected to go through during their days in Panchgani; and it treats them all, courteously but firmly, as beginners in that process.

It says that the first step – whether they are troubled by something in their own lives or worried about the way our societies are going – is to change themselves. To begin to do that, they should start with an honest and humble time of introspection, which may highlight those things which they regret about their past lives and suggest how they might make restitution for them. It might also indicate how they should change their behaviour in future.

As they listen in silence, the little yellow book tells them, they will learn to distinguish between the thoughts which come from the Inner Voice and those which are just part of the routine chatter which goes on in our heads all the time.

In their first time of quiet, it says, they should review their lives in the light of four absolute moral standards of honesty, unselfishness, love and purity, identify where they are falling short and then start to put right all they can put right.

That, moreover, is just a beginning. Then, as they make a daily practice of times of quiet, they can try to find out, with the help of the Inner Voice, what they are meant to do for their friends, their communities and their countries.

It is an exceptionally clear prospectus and it is intended for those of every faith and of none. The aim is to discover a new source of wisdom and then follow its leading. No time is wasted in the little yellow book on windy speculation or vague intentions.

There is nothing about fine thoughts, only worthwhile deeds. The focus is implacably on behaviour, although of course a person's beliefs are bound to have their impact on how he or she will judge their own behaviour. It is all very much, as the French say, *à point*. This is not just a nice little break in the mountains. The climate may be cooler than on the plains, but Asia Plateau creates its own heat by asking some disturbing questions.

All of which sounds intense and somewhat unrelenting and, in one way, it is bound to be so if Panchgani is to work any of its magic, since the average length of courses is only four days. That, however, is not what a stay in Panchgani feels like, even when people go through spiritual turbulence as the shell of self starts to crack.

For one thing, it is a strikingly beautiful place, with splendid views and groves of bougainvillea and magnolia in shady gardens; and its beauty helps time spent there feel both refreshing and full of laughter.

There are certainly plenty of light-hearted moments to irrigate the trials of personal introspection: uproarious communal tea parties where participants stand up impromptu and tell amusing stories, musical evenings put on by those who are staying there, delightful meals with companions from around the globe – a Congolese headmaster, a Tibetan hermit taking a break from his cave, Rwandans, Ukrainians, Afghans, Lithuanians, Armenians – the variety is endless.

It helps, too, that there are no gurus around, to be admired or imitated, no Holy Joes, no empty piosity. The people who live there are always ready to spend time with those who want to talk, but they do not adopt lofty attitudes.

They are only too aware of their own flawed natures and are ready to share experiences of their own weaknesses and failures if that will help.

Asia Plateau's current director is Dr Ravindra Rao, a former dentist from Bangalore and the most modest and humorous of men. He and his wife Jayashree not only give their time and services to Panchgani free, they also pay for their accommodation there. Rao is determined that the only pressure at Panchgani shall come not from human beings but from the inner voice speaking to those who come.

When I was there, he talked about wanting to create an atmosphere of non-interference. 'Pushing people,' he told me, 'is wrong'.

It is a laudable ambition and seemed to be working for many of those who were there. Tim, a young Swede in his twenties, said that there had been no pressure on him from the outside – that's to say the 'staff' – but that had only made the pressure from inside himself all the greater.

On the other hand, the frequent mention of absolute moral standards and the inner voice must make all but the most obtuse feel extremely uncomfortable, at the very least. The human conscience, when even lightly disturbed, is apt to develop its own momentum.

The fact that that process is clearly underway in so many lives, together with the unqualified openness and honesty of the people who live there permanently, has its effect on many of those who come. That is what produces the sunny faces, the friendly greetings. I have never been anywhere which has such an all-pervasive atmosphere of openness and honesty.

It is very unusual, in my experience, for the directors of a place such as Panchgani to be so open about their own most embarrassing errors. Mrs Jayashree Rao told me that, one day, she heard that one of the engineering machines her company made had yielded a profit of 100,000 rupees.

'I then got into my chauffeur-driven car,' she said, 'went shopping and bargained with a vegetable seller in the market. I managed to bring down the price by five rupees. Back in my chauffeur-driven car again, I suddenly realised what I had done. I haven't bargained since then.'

It is in the atmosphere created by this sort of honesty that the profoundly demanding and intimate processes of IoC are expected to take place, and it is in that atmosphere that they become somewhat more palatable.

All the courses at Panchgani begin with an early-morning nature walk, during which silence and nature are left to do their work. Each day the main morning meetings spell out IoC's philosophy with instances of where and how it has proved effective from the people who were involved. These meetings always end with 15 or 30-minute quiet times to let the message sink in.

On the second day, all the course members are asked to complete a three-page balance sheet. On the first page, they are asked to make a list of the people in their lives whom they have reason to be grateful to. Page two is for people they have done something to help. Page three for a list of those they may have hurt and those who have hurt them.

It is all part of a way of helping people consider their lives and identify the places where they may need to change.

Parthiban, a 64-year-old South Indian Catholic with a rollicking sense of humour is, in many ways, typical of the people who run Panchgani. He is the general manager but is clearly not an identikit executive. 'I'm not inclined to take too serious a view of things', he said. 'If you do, you start taking yourself seriously as well.'

He first came across the ideas of IoC when he was a student at the Salesian College of the Sacred Heart in Tiripattu, Tamil Nadu. At the end of his first year there, however, he failed in all his subjects. The principal, who expected a 100 per cent pass rate, was mightily displeased. He instructed Parthiban to ask his father to come to the college. As for Parthiban himself, he had best pack his bags and get ready to leave.

His father, who was both a teacher and a severe disciplinarian, lived 75 miles away. Given the circumstances, the last thing Parthiban wanted was a humiliating encounter with both his father and the principal.

Another strategy occurred to him. He went down to the bus station, where there was an old cobbler mending shoes, and offered him five rupees if he would come to the college and impersonate his father. The cobbler's clothes were not in the pink of condition, so Parthiban bought him a new shirt and dhoti and instructed him not to say too much when they met the principal.

They made an evening appointment, because Parthiban reckoned that that was a time when the principal would not be at his sharpest. However, he did not need to be at all sharp to spot the fraud immediately – because the cobbler mended his own shoes as well. Fortunately, the principal's reaction was to call in all his colleagues and tell them the story. They laughed their heads off. Parthiban was not asked to leave.

Eventually, he became so popular that he was elected president of the students' union. It was at that stage that he came across the ideas of IoC, because a travelling group were putting on one of their plays in the town. Both before and after the performance there was much talk of absolute moral standards and quiet times. Parthiban decided to experiment by having one.

At first, nothing whatever came to him but, as he walked back towards his room, the single word 'books!' popped into his mind. 'What books?', he asked himself but, when he went into his room, he was faced with all the library books he had 'borrowed', never intending to return them. There were no less than 200. They obviously had to go back to where they belonged.

But how? He was popular enough to have been elected student president but asked himself what those who'd elected him would think of him if he were to confess? Would the principal kick him out of the college? And, again, what would his father have to say?

His first inclination was that he could take the books back without making any sort of fuss, just a few at a time. But he wasn't happy with that idea, he felt he would still have been cheating. The inner voice told him to go to the principal and come clean.

So, with the help of a group of his friends – he couldn't carry all the books himself – he went to the principal's office with a good selection the next morning. The principal was busy writing his morning address, but Parthiban said he couldn't wait until the assembly was over because he wanted to confess something of which he was very ashamed.

When he had finished, the principal's reaction was something Parthiban hadn't bargained for. 'Well,' he said, 'I think you should tell the whole college about this'. So

Parthiban went with him into the assembly and told the students the whole sorry story.

He felt, he said 'like a goat waiting to be slaughtered' and as if he were making his farewell speech at the college. There was absolute silence in the hall – 'a pregnant silence at the very least', he recalled with a laugh.

During the next three days, everyone avoided him. Even his friends didn't speak to him. On the third day, the principal asked to see him. Parthiban felt sure that he was going to be kicked out but, when he went into the room, he found that all the professors and heads of department were there, together with the librarian, who actually hadn't noticed that the books were missing.

There was also, in one corner of the room, a huge pile of books stacked up against the wall. Since Parthiban had talked about absolute honesty, the principal said, 600 more books had been returned – silently. Well, thought Parthiban, I've got some company at last; and the librarian smiled at him.

This burst of painful honesty helped Parthiban practice his faith rather better. He was honest with his father and his brother, though relations were still not fully restored. When he asked his father for 100 rupees so that he might go to Panchgani, his father turned him down flat. It was already a waste of money putting Parthiban through college and he didn't want to throw any more away.

The principal, however, was convinced that Parthiban should go to Asia Plateau and gave him the 100 rupees he needed. 'Even then', Parthiban recalled, 'I was still such a crook that, when I first made the journey here, I didn't have a rail ticket. So I had to send the money back later'.

After he left college, Parthiban went to work for the India Bank, first in Delhi and then in a small village called Salem. Once there, he decided that he would start to make loans to the poorest and neediest of the locals, who wanted to start little businesses of their own as cheaply as possible. The loans ranged from 500 rupees to a million.

Parthiban's staff told him to have nothing to do with one man who turned up asking for a quite large loan. He had murdered his stepmother and spent eight years in jail. Parthiban nonetheless asked to see him. In his morning time of quiet, he had thought 'Okay, he's murdered someone, but he has served his time, so why be influenced by prejudice?'

After the man had explained in detail what he intended to do with the money, Parthiban lent him 200,000 rupees - and persuaded an insurance company to cover him against the possibility that his crops might fail. In the event, the murderer turned out to be very successful and, after some years, was elected president of the local council.

There was also in Salem a women's self-help group which was coordinated by a Muslim woman. When Parthiban discovered that she was siphoning off in commissions a sizeable percentage of the money she had raised, he was furious and shouted at her in front of the bank staff and its customers. Then he told her to get out of the bank. 'That', he thought, 'will put her straight!'

In his time of quiet the next morning, however, he thought that he had had no right to shout at the woman in front of so many people. He had the very clear thought that he needed to humble himself by apologising to her and in front of the same people. After he had done so, the woman said nothing and left the bank in tears.

Three days later, she came back and raised a loan of 9,800 rupees against the security of her jewellery. Then she used the money to repay all the commissions she had taken from those for whom she had raised money. 'She needed correction,' said Parthiban, 'but so did I.'

In the years since then, he has never lost his natural devilment. After he had left the bank to work for IoC, he went to a youth conference in Ooticamund. They all stayed in a Jesuit monastery. Nearby, there was a Salesian retreat centre for priests and nuns from which you could see marvellous views of the nearby Kottagiri Hills. Parthiban decided that he would like his whole group to go there to enjoy those views.

He called the retreat centre, but the priest he spoke to said a visit was not possible because the centre was only for priests and nuns. That didn't deter Parthiban, who declared that he was indeed a Salesian father. Well then, the priest replied, he and his group were of course welcome. When they arrived, however, the people in the retreat centre got a considerable shock. 'There were', admitted Parthiban, 'a lot of saris and not a single cassock in sight.'

The man at the door asked Parthiban whether he really was a Salesian Father. Well, he replied, I am the father of two and since I also went to a Salesian college, that makes me a Salesian father. Oh, said the man at the gate, he'd better call the Rector to try to sort out the situation.

The Rector turned out to be one of Parthiban's best college friends. 'Eh, Parthiban', he said with a smile and the whole group both saw the views and then stayed on for tea – and supper.

But what about the people who turn up at Asia Plateau for one of its courses or, indeed, for a longer stay. What are they hoping to find there – and what effect does it have on their lives? During the time I spent in Panchgani, there were none of the top Indian civil servants and businessmen who go there, though the reactions to their stay are evidently positive enough for them to go in increasing numbers.

One of the senior IAS officers who spent time in Panchgani confessed afterwards that, over a period, he had lost his enthusiasm to serve. 'Coming here.' he wrote in a letter to Rao, 'has been like wiping clean a dusty electric bulb. Now the light is shining bright again'.

And I would like to have met again Anil Swarup, the man who conceived the idea of giving Indians without health insurance a float of 30,000 rupees to spend on their family's health needs. Swarup, who often spends time in Panchgani, is delighted that his idea is now being replicated in countries across the world.

Even so, there were an extraordinary range of men and women from around the world – Burmese ministers who represent ethnic minorities, community workers from South Sudan, a lecturer in psychology from Armenia, Tibetans, Somalis, and so on.

What interested me most, though, were the young people – many of them interns who were staying in Panchgani for two or three months. Two of them, young women, were still waiting to greet me outside my room even though it was well past their bedtime, at 11.30pm.

Mostly in their twenties and early thirties, these young people clearly had not just come for a time out in a very pleasant place. All of them were trying to make up their minds what they should do with their lives. They were all looking for something larger and less selfish than a safe treadmill existence, and all those I met were ready to be spiritually radical.

'I'm at the beginning of my journey in life', said Ruta, a Lithuanian from Vilnius who has a degree in development and peace studies from Bradford University, 'and I don't know what I should do'.

She is only too aware of her country's troubled history – her great-grandfather and his family spent 18 years in a Siberian prison camp when Lithuania was part of the Soviet Union – and of its still troubled present, with Lithuania top of the league for suicides and the louring presence of the Russian bear always on the doorstep.

Some had put very promising careers on hold to be in Asia Plateau. Stephanie, an Indian Catholic software designer who loves creating new codes, had had the offer of a job with Oracle – 'the company of my dreams!' – just two days before she was due to set out for Panchgani. To the astonishment of her friends, who told her she was 'absolutely nuts', she had turned it down.

Anup, her Hindu fiancé, who has two degrees in computer engineering and business management, had also resigned from a good job despite being urged by his parents to focus on job security above all else. Previously, he had always done what his father, who works for Exxon-Mobil, advised him to do. Going to Asia Plateau he said, was the first time he had done what he himself wanted. His father, needless to say, was not best pleased.

Sabrina, who had been an intern in a big law firm in Pune, had also been told by her father that, as a girl, she must focus on earning money and building a career. By resigning and coming to Asia Plateau without even consulting her parents, she had totally ignored his advice.

'I'm selfish,' she told me, 'and although I do want to be a good daughter and to make some money, my inner voice told me to come here'.

So it is clear that these young people are not aimless drifters and certainly not no-hopers looking for a spiritual buzz. All of them had – and indeed still have – every chance of building successful careers Yet they all seemed to feel that IoC's notions of an inner voice, undergirded by absolute moral standards, was worth exploring, even at some cost. They reminded me in some ways of the Coptic Christian monks whom I had met at the monastery of St Macarius the Great in the Egyptian desert close to the border with Libya – so many of whom, to my surprise, had PhDs.

What, I wondered, had their experiment in coming to Panchgani yielded thus far? Had they come to believe in the idea of an inner voice, or did they find it merely fanciful, a figment of the imagination?

'Before I came here', said Anup, 'I always subjected every decision to logical analysis, working out the pros and cons in my mind. I'd never thought of trying to listen to the inner voice and, when I first started having quiet times, I was very confused – whatever thoughts came, I just wrote them down blindly'.

As he went on, he said, he began to sense a difference between the qualities of his thoughts. Random thoughts were lighter, more fleeting, the heavier ones – 'close to my heart' – were also more unselfish: 'I ought to do this', 'I should help these people', that sort of thing. 'It is as if a different part of me is coming alive, as if another energy is putting these thoughts inside me'. He has no doubt that such thoughts have to be obeyed.

As with so many of the other young people that energy has pointed out 'a huge list' of things in his life which needed to be put right. He was, he said, going to write to his friends who already had cars and houses and tell them honestly that he felt envious of them; to say sorry to his younger brother, of whom he had always felt jealous because their parents had never subjected him to the sort of pressure imposed on him; above all, to apologise to his father. They had had, he said, 'a very harsh' talk but the inner voice had pointed out that his father had always taken care of him.

Then there was Himanshu, a passionate young Hindu social activist of 28 who had first come to Asia Plateau in 2009 carrying a bag full of books about Communism. He'd arrived as an intern, on the prompting of an elderly friend in Lucknow, with the intention of doing nothing more than reading and eating.

'I didn't want to meet anyone or talk to anyone. I was full of hatred and I was fed up because I wasn't getting the support for my work which I had expected.

'I assumed,' he went on, 'that Panchgani was just another capitalist place, which had the aim of strengthening the existing system. I came to judge it and what they were doing here. I had won many awards for the work I had done in the villages and elsewhere, I'd appeared in the newspapers and I had lots of ego. Slowly, I began connecting with the inner voice, which told me of many things which I had been hiding. I had been fighting for unity in my country, but my sister and I hadn't spoken for ten years and I felt a great hatred against her.

'Then a charitable man had given me 5,000 rupees to buy blankets for the poor, but I had put 1,500 of that money into my own pocket. When I was honest with myself, I had to admit that 50 per cent of what I did was out of a desire to appear in the media.

'I also had great bitterness against my father. He had been a police officer but then got very badly beaten up with the result that he didn't come home again for two years. When he did, he had mental problems and used to beat me, my mother and my sister all the time. I also felt hatred for the people who had hurt him in the first place. I had a big list of things to put right.

'I started by ringing my sister and we both cried while we were on the phone. Through that crying, the hatred was washed away. Then I apologised to the man who had given me the money for the blankets. He wouldn't accept any money back, but told me that my honesty had made him feel a trust in me that he had never had before.

'I then went to the leader of our movement and told him that so much of what I had done was in the hope of getting attention in the media. He was amazed and I saw his eyes sparkle. He said 'Now we can be brothers".

Another young man told me of an experience so startling that he tells the story rarely for fear that people will think he is a little touched. His name is Mohammed Ghabris, he is 22 and a business management graduate who lives in the Hezbollah-controlled area of southern Beirut. He is the kind of young man who, you feel, has his feet firmly on the ground.

'I was here in 2014,' he said, 'and there was so much going on that I craved silence and longed to be by myself, so I went up the mountain to the plateau for three hours. At first I felt disturbed, but then the sky and the mountains gave me peace and, by the time I started walking down again, I did so with a sense of mindfulness and calm. After a while, I saw a guy in front of me and a very clear thought came to me, like a voice in my head – 'talk to him!' But then I hesitated 'shall I? . . . shall I not?' I went past him and, as I did so, he called to me and asked who I was. Then the same voice came to me again – 'he is going to ask for 100 rupees, give it to him!'. I had one 100 rupee note in my pocket. That was all the money I had.

'The man asked whether I was going to Pune. I told him that I wasn't. He said that he was going there and that he needed some money for the bus. He was, he said, 100 rupees short of what he needed. I felt like a vessel! I just took out the 100 rupee note and gave it to him. He accepted it gratefully and asked for my phone number so that he could repay me.

'When he had gone, I just knelt and cried. It was so astonishing and overwhelming, like a voice talking in my head, so insistent, so clear. I have changed my telephone number, so he couldn't ring back, but I didn't mind'.

The same kind of thing had happened to him back in Lebanon, and so he had stopped doubting that God was perfectly able to speak to us. Somehow that certainty and perhaps a greater capacity to have a listening ear had also given him a new sensitivity to people. He would think 'stop, he's feeling hurt, change the topic, he is not feeling comfortable'.

You could never tell, Mohammed went on, when the inner voice would come, but he could feel it when he was ready – 'when I'm not self-centred, when I'm not thinking of my own desires. When it comes, I feel a moment of blissfulness. I feel that there has been a symphony playing since the beginning of humanity and, when we hear that voice, we are in harmony with that music.'

'If people were to say that I'm mad, I could only reply that that is what I have actually experienced. If you are religious, you might say that that was the voice of God. I'd probably prefer Supreme Being. It's up to everyone to discover whether that is what it is. You can't find it in any book or in what other people will say to you about it.

'Even in Islam you will find imams who have only experienced the crust of religion, the superficial layer, and they will just say that what is in the book is right. (There are, I reflected, some Christian priests, who say much the same, though about a different book.) But the inner voice is something more.

'Why do they not experience it? They're limited by the words that are written. The whole experience has strengthened my faith in Islam. Why? When I was up there on the plateau, praying and talking to God, asking for strength and saying how grateful I was for all He had given me. Then that happened! I felt He was perhaps honouring me. It was a blissful moment and I felt directly connected to God'.

There are, doubtless, many ways in which one could explain Mohammed's story. Was the man simply a beggar who thought Mohammed looked like a soft touch? Perhaps. But that doesn't explain how his request exactly matched what Mohammed says he 'heard', nor does it explain Mohammed's preparedness to hand over all the money he had.

So far as Mohammed is concerned, it didn't matter. He felt he had honoured God by obeying what he was told and had been honoured in return.

Nine

Beyond Religion?

One thing that struck me forcefully about Asia Plateau was that there was scarcely any mention of individual religions, still less of their dogmas and doctrines. Perhaps that was partly because I spent most of my time talking to the younger people, who are less and less engaged with such matters. Indeed Ruta, the Lithuanian, told me that her friends and acquaintances thought that anyone who was religious was simply backward.

Yet, given that Asia Plateau is totally committed to helping people transform their lives by obedience to the inner voice, the lack of any discussion of these things seemed a little surprising.

It would be easy to conclude that the Panchgani experience is religion-lite. Yet that is plainly not the case. People such as Ruta who arrived there without the least belief in God had, after only a few weeks, become convinced that there was a God after all. She had even been to the Catholic church in Panchgani.

As a result, she told me, she was rediscovering her lost spirituality – and when she got back to Vilnius, one of the first things she intended to do was to see her Catholic priest.

Asia Plateau puts its heaviest emphasis on the need for personal change rather than persuading those who go there to sign up to a set of beliefs or doctrines.

Their conviction is that if those who come undertake the experiment of listening to the inner voice honestly – and with the stimulus of absolute moral standards – they will be obliged to face the reality of their motives, their nature and their lives in some detail.

That, in turn, will open the way for a religious experience far deeper than a superficial and emotional espousal of beliefs or practices. Open about themselves, they are more likely to be entirely open to God. They may then feel the need to go back to the religion in which they were raised, to sustain and deepen the new life that has been given to them.

That, so far as the people who run Asia Plateau are concerned, is just a beginning, as their little yellow notebook makes plain. On its cover, it declares – perhaps a touch pompously – that the purpose of what goes on there is 'addressing global needs through personal change'. It's fine, they say, if those who turn up become, through their time there, kinder and nicer, but that is not enough, it is only half the story.

The next, crucial step, is to discover, by listening to the inner voice, what they are meant to do for their community, their country, their world. Until people discovered what that was, there was a real danger that their experience would remain parochial and inward-looking. 'If we think only of ourselves', said one of the interns, Shashika da Silva, a

27-year-old Sri Lankan Buddhist, 'it is not the inner voice. The inner voice is more than conscience. It will give you a sense of direction for the future'.

Da Silva was one of the interns I met who had a clear sense of what he was meant to do when he left Panchgani. Aware of the deep divisions between his own, Sinhalese, community and Sri Lanka's Hindu Tamils, he wanted to try to play a part in healing the hatreds which have been left behind by the civil war.

His family was always urging him to find a well-paid job, but he didn't want money from anyone, he wanted to be of service. That's what the inner voice had told him. He'd already been to the Tamil heartland in the north of the island at a time when it was still dangerous to go there.

His aim was to set up a centre in the middle of Sri Lanka where Tamils and Sinhalese could work side by side, doing the practical day-to-day things together and creating theatrical shows to promote reconciliation.

Other interns were also beginning to discover what they ought to do with their lives. Jitesh, a 24-year-old Hindu had resigned a job in a software company which paid him 300,000 rupees a year and where he had a promotion on the cards; he just couldn't see himself as a 50-year-old in that company.

He'd always, he said, been a very selfish man, wanting the highest marks in school and winning the badminton matches in which he had played for the state. Now he'd been given a real sense of calling to do something for India's poor along with the friends he had made in Asia Plateau, such as Himanshu.

It would be odd if the people who run Asia Plateau didn't practice what they preach, and try to do something for their region and for India itself. Otherwise, Asia Plateau might be perceived as little more than an Oasis of the Higher Thinking.

That is what lay behind the creation of one off its offshoot called Grampari – which is simply two Marathi words – gram and pari – which mean rural economy; and its genesis owed a good deal to the shame which Jayashree Rao felt after beating down the vegetable seller in the village by five rupees.

Jayashree, who is 64 and has a smile that lights up her whole face, comes – like her husband – from a well-to-do background. Long before they married, they had given their lives to work for IoC without any salary, but had then settled down in Bangalore, where they were leading a thoroughly congenial life.

'We were both earning well', she said. 'We lived close to the Club and we had delightful Saturday night parties with our friends.' Soon, however, they both had an uncomfortable feeling that this really wasn't good enough and became increasingly convinced that they were meant to take responsibility for running Asia Plateau. That, they realised, would mean uprooting themselves from their comfortable apartment in Bangalore, but in the end they couldn't resist the gnawing conviction that that was what they were being told to do.

Soon after they arrived in Panchgani the incident with the vegetable seller made Jayashree painfully conscious that, although she realised that 70 per cent of Indians lived in villages, she knew virtually nothing about their world. She decided that it was high time she put that right. To start with, things didn't go too well. She visited four or five villages and invited people to come to Asia Plateau, in part to explain to them the government schemes that offered money to help them with their water and sanitation problems.

Much of that money, as she well knew, vanished before it reached the villages because of endemic corruption. Her invitation, however, fell on deaf ears. Almost nobody came.

She decided that she had better go back to the villages, get to know the people and find out what it was that they actually wanted. She soon discovered that what the women really longed for was the chance to earn some money.

She tried to think how that could happen and had the idea of inviting village women to come to Asia Plateau to make mud lamps, which they could then paint and sell – perhaps to the people who came to Panchgani for courses. So that they would have a place to make the lamps, she had a poultry shed on Asia Plateau's small farm converted. It was all, of course, to be free of any charge.

Her idea was an immediate hit. Around 55 women turned up. The venture also improved some of the women's domestic lives in unexpected ways. One of those who came was being regularly beaten by her husband. When she started to bring home some money, the beatings stopped.

Jayashree, however, wanted to do more than offer the women a chance to make money. She also aimed to give them a sense of empowerment, so that they felt able to play a part in running their villages. With that in mind, she showed them films in which women were doing just that. Not surprisingly, the best films had been made by left-wing political parties, so Jayashree used those.

Then, having learnt something of the harsh realities of village life, she wanted to help them discover the kind of personal change which would enable them, for example, to deal with the fights which broke out in so many villages, often between people of different castes.

So, while the women were working away at their mud lamps, she and her colleagues – she has a team of eleven, several of whom have degrees in social work – told them about the inner voice and absolute moral standards, connecting what they said with Hinduism. They spoke about the seven emotions which control us if we can't control them, taking them one by one - jealousy, anger, greed and so on.

They asked the women whether they had ever been jealous of anyone – and what effect it had had on them? They found the women only too ready to be honest about themselves and their lives. No one had ever given them the chance before. In that way, Jayashree felt that they were linking rural development and personal change in a way that was absolutely unique in India.

Often, the women brought children with them to Panchgani, and Jayashree tried to make sure they had a good time by laying on a variety of games. She also told them about the Good Voice and the Bad Voice, how they could change, how fights happened and how they could try to resolve them, about saying sorry and having a time of quiet. The children seemed to enjoy it all as much as their mothers.

Before long, Grampari was beginning to offer all kinds of things that Jayashree had never dreamt of in the beginning. In one new programme, women came to be taught skills such as sewing. Several, in due course, were able to start their own businesses as seamstresses. Asia Plateau charged 50 rupees (around £8) a session for that training, but the women were able to claim it all back in a lump sum when the festival of Divali arrived.

Then, Jayashree and her team set up what they called a livelihood programme. Each month, they invited 25 boys and girls between the ages of 16 and 20 to stay at Asia Plateau for five days to learn a variety of skills – plumbing, sewing and English-speaking. They are also, needless to say, told about the inner voice and absolute moral standards, and invited to begin having times of quiet.

'Personal change happens so naturally', said Jayashree. 'We had one boy who was a drunkard and refused to work with his father and uncle, who were fruit sellers, because he thought it beneath him. He decided to stop drinking and start working – and apologised to his father and uncle. Then there were two boys who were regarded as the thugs of the village. They decided to stop teasing girls, something which can rapidly lead to other things in this country. You should realise we are often scared when such boys come here. They are big, strong and very rough – but, in fact, they've given us no trouble.'

The youngsters don't have to pay anything like the cost of their stay. It costs Asia Plateau 13,500 rupees to have each of them, but they are asked to put down only 500 rupees. If they complete the course, they are given that money back.

There was more to come. One of the people who came to spend time at Asia Plateau was a hydrologist called Jared Sowmya. He had a special expertise in springs and decided to help local villages with any water problems they had.

In one village, the spring ran into an open pond, which let in a good deal of dirt and polluted the water. 'So we built a spring box with a filter at the back', said Jayashree, 'and that meant the water became clean. We've done springs in 25 villages so far, and each of those means clean drinking water for 500 people'.

And so it goes on, apparently endlessly. Asia Plateau offers schools a handwashing programme, and a Washing of the Heart programme, which talks about the inner voice and how to discern it in times of quiet.

Jayashree dreams of all kinds of other courses which Grampari might offer in the future. Nor, in her view, does what it offers need to be restricted to Panchgani. It could work, she thinks, in other parts of India. And, by the by, she said, she was planning to give pairs of gloves to any village women who would like them. 'You should see the state of their hands', she said with a grimace.

She feels a sense of great wonder about the way things have developed. 'It is,' she said, 'far beyond what I ever expected. And all I had to do was say 'yes' to moving from Bangalore! I wouldn't have missed this for anything'.

And what of the people who work at Asia Plateau – the cooks, those who share the wash-up with the guests, do the laundry, prepare the rooms? What do they gain apart from a living wage? Is all the talk of the inner voice just so much hot air as far as they are concerned?

There are 14 permanent *bhais* (maids) at the Centre. One of them is Kolpana Salunkhe, a Buddhist who has worked there for 28 years. She may be 'around 48 years old', she told me, cannot read or write and, when she was young, had the sort of life which made her bitter and angry for many years.

When I asked why she had been so angry, the tears began rolling down Kolpana's cheeks. 'I wanted to complete my education so much', she said, 'but my father left home for two or three years, and there wasn't enough money for any school fees. I wasn't even allowed to take any exams because we couldn't pay the fees. I never told my mother that I hadn't taken the exams, because it would have hurt her and, in any case, she couldn't have done anything about it. So at the time when the girls I knew were on their way to school, I had to go to work to earn money. When they came back and played together, I couldn't play with them because I was still at work.'

Because of these deep disappointments, Kolpana was not the easiest person to manage. She reacted fiercely to being treated as 'something below. I had a lot of fights here and in the village', she said. 'I was a rebel.' Twice she was asked to take a break from her job at Asia Plateau.

Then one of the directing staff invited her, completely out of the blue, to join the Effective Leadership course, which lasted four days. To begin with, she sat at the back of the theatre sleeping. 'I didn't know what they were talking about, I felt they were coming from a different world. The man who was speaking saw that I was sleeping and asked me to come and sit at the front. I was pleased to be asked to take the course but got absolutely nothing from it.'

One of the directing staff, a woman called Vijaylakshmi, asked Kolpana whether she had ever tried listening to the inner voice. She replied that she was quite willing to try, and they sat outside under the frangipani trees. When asked what she had heard, she replied 'only the birds'.

Vijaylakshmi asked why she didn't think about all the fights she'd had and the bad words she had used. 'In another time of quiet,' said Kolpana, 'I began to see where I had been wrong. Tears began rolling down my face and I began

134

to sob. I saw that I had been wrong in so many ways and I apologised to my mother, my neighbour and to my great aunt and uncle. I also apologised to the team here – and tried to control my temper.

'In the village, because I was known for picking fights, people used to avoid me. After listening to the inner voice, I had the idea of clearing up the area between our home and the Buddhist temple. Then I started clearing up all the rubbish which had been thrown into the fields. People in the village thought I had gone mad but soon some of them began to join me.

'After a while, I was asked if I would stand as deputy head of the village, something I'd never dreamt of. It was the young men who put my name forward. I said to the head man that I couldn't read or write, but he replied that they would handle the reading and writing if I would speak to the villagers. A lot of former untouchables live there. We've managed to do a lot of things – putting in toilets and a well.

'I love working at Asia Plateau better than being at home. I go to the temple and bow to God, but I'd do that for this place many times over. For me, the inner voice means bringing up the things which are deep within. If I hadn't learnt what I have learned from that voice, I'd never have done what I have done. I feel it is the divine, deep within.'

Ten

Silence in Singapore

So, what about my own experience of that other voice? In one way, I am loath to write about it, because it seems to be claiming some spiritual eminence or distinction which, knowing my own shortcomings only too well, would be simply ridiculous.

Yet there is no doubt that these experiences were utterly decisive in determining the course of my life, and since they steered me in what seems to have been precisely the right direction, they were gifts beyond price. Given that fact, it would be both ungrateful and churlish not to record them. So here they are – and let readers make of them what they will.

Perhaps I should begin with a little background, to show what kind of person I was when these things happened. When I arrived in Singapore in 1955 as an RAF Education Officer, I was 23 years old. I'd been to the local grammar school in Macclesfield, Cheshire, and then to Christ Church, Oxford.

There I'd picked up a decent degree (Modern History, which in those days ended in 1870!) and followed it with a year at Stanford University in California on a generous scholarship. I was offered the chance to stay on there but, partly because of a desultory and inconclusive love affair, I decided to come back to Britain to do my National Service.

In religious terms, at that time, I was a *very* nominal Christian – nominal in the sense that I had no belief whatsoever and that religion had not affected any part of my life. I had no enthusiasm for churchgoing, to the extent that I never once – in three years – crossed the threshold of the cathedral in Oxford, even though it was part of my own college.

As a boy, I'd been packed off to the Baptist chapel next door to our little grocer's shop, a couple of times every Sunday. I found it pretty tedious but then I was pretty tedious too. I used to take a handful of dried peas in my pocket and while away the time by pushing them down into my ear and then trying to prize them out again.

On one particular Sunday, when I was eight, I couldn't get the pea out again and panicked so I stood up, raised my hand and said 'Please, Sir'. 'Yes, boy,' snapped the minister, obviously not pleased to have his sermon interrupted. 'Please, Sir', I said, 'I've got a pea in my ear'. Whereupon the cleric summoned the deacons and elders, all of whom wore dark suits, and I was whisked away to the hospital to have it removed.

There was another reason for my growing dissatisfaction with the chapel. Every year, because of my parents' determination to get me out of the house as often as possible, I clocked up a near-perfect attendance at Sunday School.

The trouble was that I received exactly the same prize each year, presumably because the chapel had a large stock of them. It was a book with the title *Sanders of the River*. Sanders was, I assume, a missionary (I never actually read the book) and he was pictured on the cover, paddling a canoe up some tropical river. I didn't mind that, but I didn't want to see him again every Christmas.

I therefore moved and became a choirboy at the Anglican church up the street. It paid 2p for every attendance, which appealed to my acquisitive instincts, but the venture was not a huge success. I took to fainting whenever we knelt for prayer and had to be carted out.

Later, I went with my father to a curiously-named institution, the St Peter's Working Men's Institute, which was an adjunct of the Anglican Church across the road. There was an afternoon service every Sunday, which was attended by men who were clerks, train drivers and postmen. My own father was a boilerman and then a school caretaker.

The curious thing was that, despite all this attendance, I never once made any connection between what I heard at the services and my own behaviour, and certainly never thought there was anything amiss about the way I carried on.

Like a lot of young people at that time and perhaps even now, I lived from one day to the next, taking the hurdle of examinations as they cropped up, thoroughly enjoying playing cricket for the school and then the college. I had no idea what I should do with my life, and could not imagine being of any use to any employer.

Despite my relative success, in fact, I had very little confidence in myself. Under the surface, I also occasionally – in darker moments – had a sense that there was something missing in my life, but had no idea what it might be and certainly didn't dwell on it. If you'd asked me what it was, I probably wouldn't have thanked you for asking.

At Christ Church, there was a man who had the reputation of being an ardent evangelist and, when he appeared round the corner of Tom Quad, I scampered away as rapidly as I could. The only church service I went to in Oxford was at the Methodist chapel in New Inn Hall Street, principally because the girls were easy on the eye.

I suspect that, as an only child, I was quite remarkably self-centred and, in such dalliances as I had, I never thought of the effect of my behaviour on the lives of the unfortunate young ladies concerned. I suppose I was just a fairly normal young man.

Then came Singapore. For some, now obscure, reason, I'd offered to do an extra year, on top of my National Service, if the RAF would send me there. I still don't know why I did that, not being at all fond of the military life. Anyway, they obliged, and I was met at RAF Changi by a colleague-to-be called Jim Benson.

Jim, as it turned out, was to play a crucial part in my life. We became friends, although he did make extremely provocative remarks from time to time. He infuriated me once by asking what I wanted to do after we'd both arrived back in Britain. I replied that I'd like to work for the Manchester *Guardian*. He said: 'So you think ambition is a good thing, do you?' I hit the roof. It was just natural, I spluttered. Jim laughed and said no more.

On another occasion, he told me that he thought I was the most self-centred person he had ever met. That time, I threw a bar of soap at him, but sadly I missed hitting him.

He also tried hard to interest me in the ideas of what turned out to be IoC. I remember seeing a short film about how they – presumably with God's help – had managed to avert or solve (I can't recall which) an airline strike in America. There was also much talk of absolute moral standards – honesty, love and so on.

It all seemed thoroughly odd to me., and of no particular interest compared with cricket, where I'd just been made captain of the RAF Singapore team.

Then, one evening, he asked me whether I'd like a cup of coffee in his room. We'd done it before, so I walked into that room expecting nothing more than the usual congenial conversation – and a cup of coffee. I left the room, an hour later, with my life changed forever.

Quite suddenly, only a few sips in, Jim asked whether I would like to listen to God. An astonishing and bizarre invitation, *utterly* unexpected. I replied that there would be no point, since I didn't believe in God. Jim retorted that that didn't change God's situation at all. I didn't know what to say to that. I was stunned, embarrassed, paralysed. It was as if my will, normally in rude health, had somehow been disarmed, rendered impotent.

Since I hadn't rejected the invitation outright, Jim presented me with a blank sheet of paper and a pencil and told me to write down whatever came to me. I expected nothing but, as soon as silence had fallen, a series of thoughts of extraordinary clarity and authority poured into my mind.

The first was: 'You are a dictator on the cricket field, apologise to your team'. The second: 'When you went up to Oxford, you became a snob. Write and apologise to your parents.' The third: 'Write and apologise to the three boys you treated badly at school'.

This was astonishing in several ways. I had never consciously had any of these thoughts before, in any shape or form, but there was no doubt in my mind that they were on the button and had to be obeyed. I sensed that there was something out there which knew me far better than I knew myself and, no doubt because of all my church attendance, I instinctively gave that something the title of God.

I shared these thoughts with Jim who, so far as I can remember, made no comment – and left that room walking on air, more profoundly happy than I had ever felt in my life before. Why? I think I must have sensed that I had been given the beginnings of a different way to live, and that I was in some degree under new management.

That first quiet time had been so interesting that I couldn't wait to make the experiment again the next morning. One result was that, when I went into the Mess for breakfast, I didn't - as usual - sit silently behind the *Straits Times* but felt like saying 'Good morning' to everyone.

Looking back now, more than half a century later, I find the experience even more astonishing than it seemed at the time. After all, I'd never sat silent in my life, had less than no interest in silence and, if I'd been told about the idea before I went into Jim's room, I would have said that it was a complete waste of time.

Of course I've learned since then that the proponents of silent prayer offer people who're interested very detailed advice about how to make silence productive – sitting upright, using a prayer word or mantra to get them going, and I am sure those things can all be helpful, but I knew nothing about contemplation, meditation or, indeed, any other kind of '-ation'. Maybe it was the mention of absolute moral standards which did the trick.

I had been pushed unwillingly into silence without any warning and yet, even so, the silence had yielded instant and very precise rewards. It leads me to the conclusion that if God – and I believe it was God – can 'speak' to us so quickly, so much to the point and in such unpromising circumstances, then God can speak to anyone at any time.

The next day I started to do what I had been told to do. I wrote apologies to the three boys even though I didn't know their precise addresses – and to my parents. The next time our cricket team were together, I said – no point in muffling – that God had told me to apologise to them for the way in which I ran the squad.

They were, I think, completely astonished, and very embarrassed. They shuffled their feet but said nothing. They may have thought I was mad. Yet thereafter our relationships were transformed. There were three Australians in the team – by name King, Hanrahan and Bone. A few weeks later, Bone – who was a man of few words – said that, at first, they'd all thought it was a lot of hokum, but now they'd come to the conclusion that it was quite genuine. Perhaps as a result, they all started to address me as 'Sir' for the first time, not easy for Australians dealing with a Pom.

From that point on, life had an altogether different feel to it. Writing now, I realise for the first time – more than 50 years later – that the sense of something missing in my life disappeared, and has never reappeared. In some sense, my private and public selves became the same.

My quiet times in the early morning were never less than interesting. I wrote down the thoughts which came so I wouldn't forget them and tried to develop, during the rest of the day, what I thought of as a listening ear. I didn't want to miss anything that God might have to say to me. Thus began an intermittent conversation which, with one sizeable break, has never ended.

Clear instructive thoughts came fairly rarely, but were apt to surface at times of difficulty or anxiety. One arrived, amusingly and helpfully, in what, for me, was a rather important cricket match.

Much to my surprise, I had found myself captaining Malaya and Singapore in their match against Hong Kong, which took place over three days at the Selangor Club in Kuala Lumpur. Marvellous curries for lunch each day! Trying to be obedient, I declared early on the third day in an effort to bring the match to a definite conclusion.

This decision looked like being something of a disaster. Hong Kong needed only 30 runs and they had three wickets left. Wondering what on earth to do, a very clear thought popped into my mind: 'Put on Johnny Kirkham'. Kirkham was a good Australian medium-fast bowler. I obeyed and, obligingly, he took the three remaining wickets in very short order.

That is only part of what is, in many ways, a thoroughly comic story. As we left the field, the evening service in the Anglican church at the end of the ground began. The first hymn was 'Oft in danger, oft in woe'. The words were perfectly clear because, still being hot even at that hour, all the churches doors were wide open. At the end of the second verse came the words 'Know ye not your Captain's power?'

I burst out laughing. God, I thought, obviously has a very good sense of humour – and, if this doesn't sound entirely deranged, I fancied that I then heard the sound of laughter in heaven.

'A God who is interested in the result of cricket matches!' spluttered a good friend when he heard the story recently. 'It's a parody of the Sunday School image of God.'. Of course, he is absolutely right, it is a preposterous story but I'm afraid that is how it was.

There were still a number of other, quite remarkable, experiences of the inner voice to come. I had decided to 'give my life to God', which meant leaving to Him the big decisions which still lay ahead: what career should I follow, who – if anyone – should I ask to marry me. The career issue proved rather trickier than I might have hoped. Obedience to what the inner voice had to say was sometimes by no means easy.

Back in Britain and shortly to come out of the RAF, I had to find myself a job. This was the end of the 1950s and, if you had a decent Oxbridge degree, jobs fell off trees. My memory is that I had three offers – the first to become a management trainee at the BBC, the second to join the Confederation of British Industry's North American department, the third to start at the *Scotsman* newspaper in Edinburgh as a trainee sub-editor.

The first two were, of course, in London, on decent salaries and with obvious prospects. The job at the *Scotsman* was on the minimum National Union of Journalists salary, then £600 a year, and Edinburgh seemed rather far away from where ambition might have led me.

That was my state of mind when, in my last days in the Air Force, I went to see a totally absorbing film, *Bridge over the River Kwai*. Suddenly – and it is the only time in my life that it has ever happened – something very like a voice told me: 'I want you to be a journalist'. It was so like a voice, indeed, that I looked round to see if one of the audience had spoken. Nobody had. They were all watching the film intently.

Not being entirely devoid of the ambition my friend in Singapore had observed, I hoped that this would not end by my going off to Scotland. In truth, in an effort to try to avoid that possibility, I recruited a group of friends who also practised the idea of listening to the inner voice, to help me decide what God wanted. They proved wholly unhelpful to my desire to avoid the *Scotsman*. I thought at least one of them might say, for example, that the BBC was a far more strategic place to be, but nobody did.

After we had sat in quiet together, every single one of them had the thought, in various forms, 'Graham will know'. As for me, I had the thought that Edinburgh was where I should be heading. Disappointing but decisive.

Then came what was almost the hardest part – the simple act of putting into a postbox my two letters of rejection to the BBC and the CBI. The postbox was only 20 yards away from our terraced cottage in Macclesfield. They were the longest 20 yards of my life. I hesitated for several moments before dropping the letters in. As I walked back home, I wondered if I'd just thrown away two glorious career opportunities. As it turned out, God had put my unwilling feet on what seems to me now precisely the right road.

That realisation illustrates, as forcibly as anything could, the crucial importance of obedience to the inner voice when a powerful inner instinct has been endorsed by trusted friends.

The years in Edinburgh were a delight. My new colleagues were, without exception, very good to work with. I also found myself in a most attractive city where servers in cafés told you what *not* to choose from the menu.

The only disappointment was that, towards the end of my time there, I received what I have come to regard as a Scottish pay increase. When I asked the editor whether I might be worth a raise, he replied that, although it was of course a privilege to work for the *Scotsman*, he thought I might merit in increase. I didn't dare to say 'how much then?' I had to wait until the next pay slip arrived. When it came, I found that it was a measly £10 a *year!*

Perhaps understandably, I wondered if a move south might not be a good idea and was offered a place as a feature writer on the newly-launched *Sunday Times* colour magazine. By that time I was 29 and beginning to wonder if I ought to think about getting married.

There were, however, no obvious candidates and no promising romances. The only girl on the horizon was Jean Forster, whom I'd first met at primary school, when we were both only four years old. The problem was that I was not in love with her.

In the years before I went to Singapore, we'd seen each other from time to time, played tennis and danced together, but nothing more than that. I had never kissed her, nor indeed thought of doing so. When she got engaged to someone else while I was in Singapore, however, I did feel a certain annoyance. Why, I couldn't have told you. It was as if someone had infringed on my turf.

By the time I came back to Britain, Jean's engagement had ended, most hurtfully, just a week before her wedding. Her husband-to-be had gone off with someone else.

There was another factor. It had become fairly clear that Jean's mother, Elizabeth, wanted me to marry her daughter. She and my father worked in the same mill, and she thought well of him. But, though I admired and respected Jean, I could not avoid the fact that I was not in love with her and therefore in no position to go further. I became increasingly uncomfortable.

What on earth to do? All I could think of was to put the whole thing in God's hands, to ask Him to do something that I could not do for myself: actually fall in love with her. At the time, I was in digs in Harpenden. For three nights before I turned in, I got on my knees, told God what the problem was, and that I could not honourably propose to Jean until I had somehow fallen in love with her. I simply couldn't manage it on my own. It was up to Him.

To my utter astonishment, my prayers were answered, and in quite short order. A couple of weeks later, Jean came down to London to see me and other friends. I waited for her train on the platform at Euston. I had no idea what was going to happen. What *did* happen was that I knew, immediately, as soon as she stepped off the train, that I felt completely differently about her. Somehow, what I had asked for, had happened and there was absolutely no mistake about it.

It was obvious what I ought to do – 'propose'! So I did so, right there on the platform. Jean said 'yes' and we celebrated by sharing a British Rail meat pie.

People may well say that I had consciously or sub-consciously willed myself into it. I would reply that the magic of being in love with someone is not something you can talk or will yourself into, particularly if you have felt no physical attraction for the person. In any case, we were very happily married for 52 years. Jean was the most magnificent of wives.

There came a time, though, fairly early in our marriage when I deliberately deserted the inner voice. I stopped having quiet times and made the advancement of my career my top priority. That was after I'd joined the BBC and become a reporter and then their first economics correspondent, although I knew next to nothing about economics.

The result was all too predictable. I started losing my temper with my three children – my son Patrick labelled it my 'horridability' – whenever they disturbed my writing. I also started to fiddle my expenses.

Each Monday morning, my secretary would ask how much I wanted for the past week and I would nominate a figure which bore no relation to what I had actually spent. There were several lunches with the Chief Secretary to the Treasury that never took place.

I did the same with my taxes. I also had a mild flirtation with someone in the office, which could have gone much further but fortunately didn't, partly because I wasn't able to carry disloyalty that far. I didn't even kiss her, but I did fantasise about taking her to Paris.

Luckily my friends in IoC kept in touch with me, and as time went by, I gradually became fed up both with myself and with the way I was living. One day, one of those friends invited me to an egg-and-bacon lunch at his flat, and afterwards suggested that we might have a quiet time.

The invitation fell on fertile soil. I was so dissatisfied with myself that I readily agreed. It was almost a relief to have the chance to open myself to whatever God might have to tell me.

The inner voice seemed to have been waiting for a chance to be heard. Four thoughts came very quickly, and they made it plain that there was no painless way back.

'Go to the taxman and tell him you have been fiddling your taxes: get in touch with the director-general of the BBC and tell him that you have been cheating on your expenses; tell Jean about the other woman' and, fourthly, 'apologise to your neighbour for building an extension which reduces his sunlight, and which you never even asked him about'. Oddly enough, I felt more relief than fear when it was plain what I had to do. I had no idea what the cost, in all senses, was likely to be, but there was no alternative – in my mind at least – to simple obedience. By that time, incidentally, I had left the BBC, so going to see the DG was a little less challenging than it might have been had I still been working there.

I drove home, knowing that I had to tell Jean everything. The hardest thing was to be honest about the other woman, because I knew that Jean had always been totally loyal to me. I wept as I told her. Being Jean, she forgave me immediately.

When I told her that I had to come clean with the BBC about my expenses, she was perfectly happy with my doing that. It was when I told her that I had to go and see the Inland Revenue about cheating on my taxes that she became thoroughly alarmed.

'You can't do that!', she said. 'You'll go to jail.' A mayor of our home town, Macclesfield, had suffered that fate for the same sin, and I think a newspaper headline must have flashed into Jean's mind: 'BBC's former economics correspondent a tax fraud'.

I had never before gone against Jean's advice on anything major, but this time I felt I had to. It was a miserable journey driving over to the Revenue's office in Aylesbury. The poor taxman who met me had no idea why I wanted to see him and, when I confessed what I had been doing, he went as white as a sheet and said: 'We have no procedure for this.'

He soon recovered, however, and told me that I was, of course, guilty of fraud, which hurt. On the way back home, with my tail firmly between my legs, I said plaintively to God: 'I'm, being a good boy, why do I feel so utterly miserable?' The answer came back instantly: 'You have to pay.'

In the end, my dealings with the Revenue ended happily. I seem to remember that I paid back around £1,000 – which in 1970 was a substantial sum. Generously, the Revenue spared me jail and only levied a £50 fine. When I went back to Aylesbury to learn my fate, the story must have been told round the building, because everyone I met greeted me as if I were the Prodigal Son.

Going to see the Director-General of the BBC, Charles Curran, was altogether easier. Charles happened to be a Catholic and understood confession. I offered £1,000 in restitution, which was just my best estimate of what I had stolen.

'Well, Graham,' he said, 'we always thought that we underpaid you, so we'd like you to regard that as a delayed pay increase.' It was typical of Charles, thoroughly generous, but it didn't seem to me to meet the case. 'I'm sorry, Charles,' I said, 'but I really feel I need to pay the money back.' 'Very well,' he replied, 'it will go into the War Memorial Fund.' I did not know what that was, but it seemed entirely suitable.

Those repayments totally cleared out our savings and since, by then, we had two children at fee-paying schools, it was not the best time to be broke. Again, painful obedience seemed to bring its own rewards. Later the same year, out of the blue, I won two literary prizes which more than covered what I had paid back. It sounds almost too pat, doesn't it, but perhaps I may be forgiven for imagining that a loving God was somewhere in the picture.

Then, in trying to find a new way forward in life, I received vital help from a most surprising source.

Before I left the BBC in 1970, I had already sought – and been offered – a job with Royal Dutch Shell. At that point, I was also writing a book, part of it about the extraordinary financial skills of a man called Jim Slater. Slater ran a bank called Slater Walker, and he was the City whizz-kid of his day.

We drove down to Devon together in his Bentley, with the idea of working on my book. On the way, Slater asked what I was proposing to do after the BBC, and I told him I was going to Shell.

At that, he exploded with disbelief and disapproval. 'That is absolutely the wrong thing to do,' he declared. 'You are NOT a corporate man.'

Nor did he leave it at that. For the whole of our time in Devon, he kept on insisting that I must change my mind. No evangelist could have been more ardent or persistent. The book was all but forgotten.

I was astonished by Slater's obvious concern for me – something entirely new in our relationship, which had previously been nothing more than business-like. As this relentless bombardment continued, I told him that I couldn't possibly make a decision as big as this without talking to my wife Jean. Fine, Slater replied, he'd speak to his wife Helen and we would all have supper together. He booked a table at a small restaurant in Surrey and Jean drove over from Oxford to meet us there. Unbelievably, when we arrived, we found that there was just one other diner – the man who had hired me for Shell.

When I whispered to Slater who the man was, he couldn't believe it either. He asked the waiter to give us a table as far away as possible, but even then our discussion about whether I should decide not to go to Shell had to be somewhat sotto voce.

Slater then addressed my anxieties about the alternative – becoming a freelance journalist – quite directly. He would, he said, guarantee to pay me the same salary as Shell were offering – £6,500 pounds – for five years, though if I earned more than that, he would take 30%.

So, next day I swallowed hard and telephoned Shell to tell them that I would not, after all, be joining them. They didn't seem at all put out. Much better to decide before you actually came, replied the man form Shell. So that was that. A couple of days later, having thought about it, I thanked Slater for all he'd done but said that I had decided not to accept his offer. Much better, I felt, to be my own man.

Very well, he replied, but I've given you three days of my valuable time, so now you can come and work for me for three days, which I did. When he asked what I would have charged him for the work I'd done had he been employing me, I said a hundred pounds a day, which seemed to me to be quite hefty for 1970.

Slater shook his head. Far too little, he said. I should have asked at least £1000. Never undercharge yourself again. That, too, proved to be very good advice.

What had never occurred to me during this entire episode was that in seeking work with Shell, I was deserting the calling God had given me years before, to be a journalist. Jim Slater was the unlikely instrument who was used to guide me most unwillingly,, back to that calling. That, to me, is the truly extraordinary and wonderful thing about the whole episode.

In those fraught and worrying months, when so much in my life was being turned upside down, there were other – non material – benefits which were quite beyond price.

Our son Patrick was seven at the time, and I felt that he was old enough to understand what was going on. I told him I was paying the money back. 'Well', he replied, 'if you'd been honest in the first place, you wouldn't be in trouble now'.

Thank you, I thought. That, however, was not the end of the story. Five or six weeks later, he came downstairs one morning looking thoroughly unhappy. I asked what was troubling him. With great difficulty, he said: 'I have been stealing sweets from the local shop.'

I was stunned. Jean and I regarded Patrick as a model child, a candidate for the mayor of some great city almost from birth. What did he think he should do about it, I asked? 'God has said to me that I should pay the money back,' he replied, 'all the money I've got.'

'How much do you have?', I asked. '30p', he replied. Well, I said, it would be wonderful if he could do that some time. No, said Patrick, he had thought that he should do it on the way to school that same morning. The local shop was owned by an elderly Catholic called Mr Gotelier and Jean told me that, when Patrick admitted that he had been stealing sweets, and held out his 30p, Mr Gotelier broke down in tears.

'I can't take your money,' he said. 'But you must', replied the little boy. 'God has told me to give it to you.' That, as it has turned out, was the beginning of a profound faith which has always been based on simple reality.

Readers may put all kinds of constructions on the events I have described but, for myself, I have no doubt whatever that there is a loving God who can lead us when we are willing to be led.

There is a Christian hymn which contains the rather un-poetic line in its fourth verse: 'Experience will decide.' It is on the basis of experience that I believe what I do.

Eleven

Inklings

I once talked with Father James McCaffery, a distinguished Carmelite monk of many years, about his prayer life. After he'd told me, in frank and impressive detail, I said that my own practice – which I had never thought of as prayer – was to have a time of quiet each morning. In that time, I made myself open to God should He have anything to tell me and with a willingness to obey anything that seemed to come from Him.

I'd been doing that, I told Father James, for the best part of half a century. To my complete surprise, he replied: 'But that, of course, is the highest form of prayer.'

Having been brought up to think of prayer as us talking to God, I had never thought of 'listening' to God in silence as prayer. In fact, I'd never have tried to do any such thing if I hadn't been muscled into it by my friend Jim.

Once I had tasted the bracing power of what came in silence, however, I never thought twice about surrendering my life to whatever came from that mysterious source which I called God. That first experience had been so unexpected and so utterly compelling that there seemed no other reasonable choice. But was what I did in my time of quiet really 'prayer'? Father James's words made me think again.

The dictionary definition of prayer, as I discover, is 'a solemn request for help or an expression of thankfulness to God or another deity' which, on the face of things, does still sound very much like us talking to God.

On the other hand, asking God for anything He might have to say to us in obedient silence, with absolute moral standards as a constant benchmark is surely as solemn a request for help and guidance as one can imagine. So, yes, perhaps Father James was right and what I had been doing for all those years was praying even though I didn't speak at all. Not that I'm against spoken prayers. Indeed I say my prayers every night.

When my first wife Jean was in a care home after a complicated series of illnesses, I asked what she had thought of the early morning times of quiet that we shared for decades. I wanted to know what she felt about them before she died. It was almost as if she had been waiting to be asked.

'Having a quiet time', she replied without the least hesitation, 'is for me a cry for help and a cry for safety – safety from the unknown, safety from anything you are afraid of. That is because there is something in the silence which has a wisdom far greater than our own. It is something beyond ourselves, not just the logic we use when we work things out – an extra element'.

I noticed, I said, that she hadn't chosen to call that something God, even though I knew she was a convinced Christian. 'Well.' she said, 'you are never quite sure where these things come from. It is a mystery. It is just my experience that, through times of quiet, we can tap into a wisdom much greater than our own.'

'That wisdom is sometimes a surprise and sometimes gives you insight into somebody else and their problems, as well as difficulties you are having yourself. In those cases, I first ask for His help, but I have no demand because I really do believe that God knows best.'

Then she added: 'I'm sure there is some connection between obedience – our willingness to obey what we are given in quiet – and the fact that it then opens a door to another kind of life than the one we have been leading. And that's not just trying to be good, it's living on completely different lines, it's relinquishing your claim on things, giving up ownership of your life.'

Those who practise this sort of quiet time are hoping for far more than peace of mind, precious though that is. They are hoping for more than being able to free their minds of mental clutter and anxiety, precious though that is.

What they are hoping for is clear direction from and a sense of fellowship with the higher power in which they trust and believe. Implicitly, they are surrendering their wills to that power.

C. S. Lewis describes the process splendidly in his book *Mere Christianity*. 'The real problem of the Christian life,' he writes, 'comes the very moment you wake up each morning. All your wishes and hopes for the day rush at you like wild animals. And the first job consists simply in shoving them all back, in listening to that other voice, taking that other point of view, letting that other larger, stronger, quieter life come flowing in. And so on all day. Standing back from all your natural fussings and frettings, coming in out of the wind.'

I have always been intrigued by what people I know have received from that other voice in their times of quiet. Often their initial experience seems to have been very simple, perhaps only one thought.

'I was fascinated by the idea of quiet times,' Omnia Mazouk, a Muslim whose father was then the Egyptian Ambassador in Australia, told me, 'and, when I tried one, I expected to be given great thoughts about the world. Instead, I was told to apologise to my father for stealing money from his desk and to my brother for feeling jealous of him because he is so charming and lively.' Omnia is now a consultant paediatrician in the north of England.

'I had my first quiet time when I was 18,' recalled Dr John Lester, a retired physician whose grandfather was a president of the Methodist Conference, 'and only one thought came to me: "You cheat when you are playing tennis with your sister". Jill was younger than me, she had a lot of talent and I just couldn't bear to be beaten by her. When one of her shots fell on the base line, I always called "out"! So I had to apologise to her. That thought was an eye-opener to me. I don't know what made me think of it, but it made me realise just how strong the competitive urge is in me.' Are these simple promptings just the work of conscience or is there a divine rationale behind them? That is more than possible because I have been impressed by how often obedience to these promptings have helped the people involved find faith, direction and a way to unravel the tangled skein of their lives.

Ramez Salamé came from a Maronite Christina family in the Lebanon but had become an agnostic at the age of 14.

As a result, any interest he had had in religion disappeared entirely.

Then, after starting to study law, he became friends with two young men from England and Australia. He met them two or three times a week in a local café or club – his father was a successful businessman – and he was particularly struck by their honesty, their willingness to confess when they had done something wrong.

He soon realised that their honesty had something to do with the quiet times which they spoke of and, almost by osmosis, slipped into the habit himself. One morning, he had what he calls 'a very clear thought': 'You are neglecting your two sisters. Do something for them.' What on earth could he do, he asked himself? The answer was, 'Take them to the cinema. They cannot go alone and that is what they would love to do.'

'When I actually did so', Salamé said, 'it was a first victory over the total self-centredness in which I had been living. After that, I found myself able to do things I'd never have dreamt of doing before. I may have been reading law, but at that time – 1968 – there were no books. The professors would speak quickly and we were supposed to write it all down as fast as we could.

'One morning, a fellow student came to me and said that he had to go away for three days and would I do a carbon copy of my notes for him? Before, I would never have agreed but this time I immediately said yes. I was astonished at myself. Somehow, *un souffle d'amour* had come into my being'.

When civil war broke out in Lebanon, Salamé risked his life to try to bring reconciliation between his own side and the Muslims. That is a perfect illustration of what Richard Chartres, the Bishop of London, once said to me: "If you start honestly anywhere, you will be led everywhere.'

That everywhere, though, may demand further acts of obedience on the way. John Lester's marriage is a case in point. He had duly apologised to his sister Jill, who seems to have been rather startled since she had no idea that he had been cheating – and then continued having times of quiet.

When he was 21 and in his third year of medical training, he woke one morning with the thought, 'One day you will marry Elizabeth McCall.' It seemed to drop, ready-formed, into his mind. It came, he told me, totally out of the blue. He had seen Elizabeth in London but never thought 'now there's a girl I'd like to marry'.

He also had a second thought, equally clearly, 'but not yet!'. To John, that meant that he ought not to take his first thought any further for the time being. He just had to accept, as best he could, that God would give what He had promised in His own good time.

In the years that followed, the idea that he would one day marry Elizabeth never left him. Whenever he saw her in London, his pulse rate quickened but he never sought her out or tried to get to know her. He was trying to obey the spirit as well as the letter of what he felt God had told him.

Such relationship as they did have was sometimes rather cool. Elizabeth had taken a secretarial course and once, when she had typed a couple of letters for him, he asked her to do the envelopes as well. 'I'm afraid I don't have time for that', she replied briskly.

Several years went by, John qualified as a physician and began working between 90 and 100 hours a week as a junior doctor in one of the big Birmingham hospitals. He had no further thought from God about Elizabeth and, as time went by, began to wonder how marriage to her would ever come about. He was tempted to 'do things in the usual way' and went out several times with another girl, but never quite lost a sense of curiosity that he should just be leaving it to God.

When he was 25, John felt that God was asking him to give up his work as a doctor and, instead, become a full-time worker with IoC, which he knew carried no salary of any kind. He had loved being a doctor and could not understand why he kept getting the thought, again and again, to give it up. He asked God why on earth He was asking him to walk away from medicine, for which he had trained so long and hard.

The reply was that, if he was unwilling to obey what was being asked of him, it would show that his medical work had become his own possession rather than God's. So, most reluctantly, John obeyed.

Once he had made that decision, he soon had the thought that now was the time to go ahead with the belief that Elizabeth was meant to be his wife. He decided that he wouldn't 'do it in the world's way' by trying to get to know her but, instead, just tell her what he felt about her. So he arranged to see her in one of the homes in London which IoC had at that time.

Elizabeth was handling IoC's telex traffic and assumed that that was why John wanted to see her. At that point, she had two lists in her mind of men she might marry, one short, the other long, probables and possibles, but John wasn't on either list.

Despite the existence of the lists, she also wasn't desperate to get married. 'If you've given your life to God, as I had', she said, 'you just want to do His will'. Only two months before John asked to see her, she had decided that one of those on her list of whom she had begun to feel fond was not the man for her. Any feelings she had had for him simply faded away.

She began to feel suspicious and uneasy when she discovered that John did not want to see her about telexes. When she found that a fire had been lit in the room where they were to meet, she thought 'on dear!' John was nothing if not straightforward. He simply said: 'I love you very much and I would like to ask you to marry me.'

It was, she said, a big shock but not a nasty one. Her list of possible marriage candidates went through her mind, with John nowhere on it and she said she needed time before responding. She didn't feel anything for this man. How was she to know what to do? John was perfectly happy to leave it there, but Elizabeth thought it would be sensible to at least get to know him a little before they parted.

As they talked, they discovered that both their families had medical backgrounds and Elizabeth had a growing sense of 'just being myself with John. I didn't have to be more than I was, it was all totally natural'. By this time it was late in the afternoon, so she offered to make a cup of tea before going off to think about what to say to John.

She spoke to two close friends and then had a time of quiet alone. By this time, she had begun to like John but, not surprisingly, had no sense of being in love with him. Then came a very clear thought: 'This is a gift that I want you to accept. If you do, I will give you all you need.'

Until that time, she said, she had had no need to trust God totally but now she again gave her life to Jesus and asked John to come over to see her. 'I knew I had to do what I had been told, so – having been honest with John about her two lists – I said that I had had this very clear thought and so I would like to say yes.'

Once she had said yes, Elizabeth felt a huge sense of excitement. She rang her parents, who were delighted. She realised that John could not have proposed at a better moment. Had he asked two months earlier, before she had given up her affection for the other man, she would have been in a dilemma. As it was, the timing was perfect.

She and her friends had been planning a party for a bunch of teenagers on the following evening. That quickly turned into an engagement party, at which she and John were able to tell their story.

When the teenagers had gone, Elizabeth suddenly felt an overwhelming sense of love for John. God's promise that He would give her all she needed had been fulfilled. It showed her, she said, that He knew what He was doing.

'People can say that I was just desperate to get married, but I was really trying to follow God as meaningfully as I could and, all of a sudden, I felt I was walking along a path not of my own making. It was like following a guide rather than charting my own path. That may sound silly or banal, but it was very real. I felt that God was embracing the two of us, that John was a person I wanted to be with always.

'I've found the same thing as life has gone on. I've been led in certain directions, I've obeyed and, again and again, it has worked out. Often God asks you to take a difficult step then He gives you what you need. If you proceed in obedience, things work out and open up again and again. It really is quite persuasive that there is something there'.

'It is a difficult thing to explain convincingly to someone who knows nothing of God', said John, 'and you could say that I was, and am, a credulous ass. But, just like Liz, my experience has been that, when I have trusted God, He has never let me down.

'If that happens once, that's one thing but, if it happens again and again, your sense of certainty grows. If other people think this is all rubbish, so be it – but it'll never be rubbish to us'. All I can say is that John and Liz, both now in their seventies, are one of the happiest and most unselfish couples I have ever met.

One of the results of trying to follow the leading of that other voice is that that growing sense of certainty helps to create a faith which can be remarkably robust because it is not based purely on belief but on concrete experiences of God's wisdom and love. Once you have had, in my own case, just one of those experiences, you no longer have any doubt that God, in whatever form, is a reality.

Being particularly fond of food, my mind instinctively battens onto food metaphors. Once you have tasted a banana, you no longer have the least doubt that bananas do actually exist.

I have never thought of myself as a person of great faith. That is for people who are far more spiritual than I have ever been. Yet my wife Jean and I learnt a good deal about our own faith when my younger daughter Hannah was thrown by a horse at the age of 11 and became desperately ill.

She was hydrocephalus from birth – a condition in which fluid accumulates in the brain, enlarging the head and often causing brain damage unless a way of draining the liquid away is found. In her case, that involved fitting a plastic shunt behind her ear and under the skin when she was only 18 months old. The fall from the horse onto her head had clearly infected the shunt and meant that a replacement had to be fitted.

We were lucky to be allotted a brilliant brain surgeon on the NHS, Chris Adams, and he began trying to fit a new shunt which would drain the liquid from Hannah's brain. It turned out to be a long, fraught process. Chris would fit a new shunt, but then it would become infected and start leaking again. That happened four times, often enough for my wife and I to wonder whether it was ever going to work.

By that time, Hannah had lost not only a great deal of weight – she was down to four stone at one point – and, of course, most of her hair. Her spirits, not surprisingly, were often low; and the boys from her class at school put together a whole book of messages to try to cheer her up. There were many, many moments when both we and she despaired of a good outcome.

Jean and I often wept on each other's shoulders when we saw her plight and, as failure followed failure, Hannah too, though wonderfully courageous, began to lose hope. One night, I left her hospital room about nine in the evening and then had to go back because I'd forgotten to give her something.

I found her sobbing her heart out, with her face turned towards the wall so that nobody would hear. Sadness overwhelmed me and I wept with her.

At about this time, one of the ward sisters, Debbie, Hannah's favourite nurse, asked Jean and me whether what was fast becoming a desperate situation did not affect our faith. Both of us replied that it didn't. Indeed, we were rather surprised to be asked the question because, when we had thought about it, the issue had never crossed either of our minds.

It may sound unfeeling but, despite all our tears and prayers, we were so accustomed to trying to hear that other voice and to obey it, that God was very real to us and we'd had such experience of His wisdom and love that, whatever the outcome had been, we could not imagine that love coming to an end.

Chris Adams himself must sometimes have wondered if he was going to succeed with Hannah, though he never communicated that doubt to us, and, refusing to be beaten, he fitted a new shunt for the fifth time. This time, there was no leakage for several days and we became so optimistic that we decided we might go down to Devon to try to build up Hannah's strength again.

For several days, everything went swimmingly. The sun shone, Hannah ate everything we set before her and she slowly began to pick up strength and happiness. Then, one dreadful morning, yet another setback: we discovered that the shunt had started leaking again. There was nothing for it but to pack up as fast as we could and hurry back to Oxford.

So we were back to square one but unbelievably, when Adams fitted another new shunt – the sixth operation Hannah had had in only eight weeks – it did not become infected and it did not leak. Hannah came home again and, as morning after anxious morning passed, and all had gone well, we began to feel that the apparently impossible had come to pass.

Hannah remembers her mother saying to her: 'God has given you a second chance' and thinking about those words, she says, that was the moment when her own faith really started to grow.

There were no other problems until Hannah was 22, when she had to have the shunt replaced again. By that time, she had a job and, as Adams had always promised, was leading a perfectly normal life.

Then in 2009 when she was 40, and having married a Kenyan called Fred five years before, she decided that she was going to walk the full length of the British Isles, from John O'Groats to Lands End with only her dog Ben for company. She wanted, she said, to get to know Britain better and felt that she desperately needed a new challenge.

Jean and I were astonished and more than a little anxious, but felt we could not tell her not to do it. It took Hannah three months, but she did it. Every day, rain or shine, she put her best foot forward and, she says, 'every mile was worth it'. Hannah is now 48, lives in Cheshire and is a dog walker. Her company name is Wag 'n Wheel, because she takes the dogs walking with the aid of a mobility scooter, the result of carrying too much dog food with her on the long walk.

But what, you may well ask, would have happened to this wonderful faith of yours if Hannah had died? I cannot, of course, know for sure but I'm as certain as I can be, that it would not have been shaken, inconsolably sad as we would have been to lose her.

For one thing, neither Jean nor I ever had any time for the 'you-scratch-our-back, God and we'll scratch yours' version of religion when 'belief', if that's what it is, depends on things going well and a decent dividend rolling in return for one's 'faith'. Tragedy strikes, as it does for all of us, and in so many forms, and then the inevitable question comes, 'Where were you God?'

There's nothing intrinsically virtuous about the faith that Jean and I were given, but we were both aware that our marriage was the result of what we regarded as God's intervention; and we couldn't imagine that such a God would suddenly cease to exist simply because we were grieving for the death of our daughter. That other voice was far too real to us for us to not give it pride of place in our lives.

My own daily practice, for what that is worth, is very simple. I use no mantra, say no special prayer but I am, metaphorically, on my knees. I follow the advice of Rowan Williams, who says that 'a morning meditation need not be in any way complicated or mystical. We need to realise that the presence of God is as all-pervasive as the air we breathe'.

I sit in silence and write down the thoughts which come to me, so that I don't forget them. Sometimes, there are many, sometimes few. As Edmund Newey, the sub-dean of Christ Church, Oxford, once said to me 'the Holy Spirit is not at your beck and call'. If that Spirit chooses to communicate with us in some way, that is the most precious of gifts. We belong to God and not the other way around.

Am I totally deluded, chasing moonbeams and giving them the name God? Perhaps. Yet I have lived for the last half century and more on the basis of obeying the thoughts which came to me in the early morning and at other times of day. My son Patrick once said to me: 'God loves attention and obedience is a very special kind of attention'.

In my experience, the thoughts came in various vocal weights, if I can put it like that. There are thoughts for friends, letters to write, telephone calls to people who are having a hard time, apologies to make for my own bad behaviour.

There are gentle admonitions, fierce admonitions. Sometimes, at worrying or puzzling times, there have been thoughts of ringing reassurance about what life is about to offer. 'All will be well! All', came the thought recently, again and again.

Always preparing myself mentally in case that didn't happen, I hesitated to believe what I was being told. When everything *did* work out astonishingly well, I duly gave thanks to God. Immediately, the thought popped into my mind: 'Well, what did I tell you?'

Some of the things that I write down concern things to be done and have nothing remotely spiritual about them. Others seem to come from a different place and have a curious authority about them. They are not the product of my normal thought processes.

There was one occasion, long ago, which more than any other, mystified me and still does. We were on holiday in Devon, the children were swimming and I suddenly became aware that my son Patrick, who was then about 12, was worried about something. 'I've lost my glasses', he shouted.

I waded out to try and help him find them, but, in those grey waters, neither he nor I could see a thing. For 15 or 20 minutes we fumbled about nervously with our feet, not wanting to tread on the glasses, but we found nothing. I wondered if we were even looking in the right place. In desperation, I said to God: 'Please show us where those glasses are.'

An answer came immediately and with astonishing precision: 'Move your left foot slowly to the left'. I did exactly that and my foot made a gentle contact with the rather flimsy spectacles. It seemed like a minor miracle; I could not begin to explain it except in terms of God's kindness.

Those morning quiet times are, for me, the beginning of a conversation which goes on all day – with me asking for the Spirit's presence or help in what I should do or how I should be. I may have been following that practice for a long time but what comes out of them so often remains a mystery and, in trying to discern that other voice, I am a perpetual novice.

John Lester believes that one of the virtues of having regular quiet times is that they give God a chance to mould us, to show us where and how we need to be different. None of it is a matter of technique, there is no approved method and everyone who values morning meditation goes about it differently. When he told me about it in Cambridge, Rowan Williams' practice rang many bells.

'First thing in a morning, 7-ish,' he said, 'having got up and had a wash, I sit or squat on a little stool and say the Jesus prayer – "Lord Jesus Christ, son of God, have mercy on me, a sinner". I repeat that prayer many times.

'In those minutes, I'm not thinking of anything in particular. I'm not consciously laying problems before God. I'm slowing down my ordinary responses, relaxing a bit and, in that framework, a thought may come to the surface. I won't be trying to think through a problem that I'm having to deal with, but there may come a moment where I can say 'ah yes!'

'In what I do each morning, I'm simply putting myself before God and saying 'this time is yours, I'm here, you will know what to give me". I said that, in the years when he was Archbishop, he must often have begun his time of quiet feeling somewhat burdened. Williams simply covered his face with his hands but made no comment.

The he went on: 'Yes, on some mornings you may be burdened but you are still less likely to be caught up in a chain of thinking. All manner of things may float around in your mind, flecks of fantasy left over from the previous day, but you've not got started with the specific worries of the new day.

'This kind of meditation is very much in the eastern Christian tradition, but I've had a lot of help from Buddhists in focussing on these things. Now it's as much a matter of routine as eating breakfast. The benefit of doing it is that I've anchored the day in the place where I need to be.

'Without it, I haven't dropped anchor. If I've missed having those minutes in the morning, I know that, if I've got any sense at all, I'll find time for it later in the day. Not doing it is starving oneself of something that will bring us truly alive.

'Mind you, there is a cross-over moment – OK, I'm doing this because it helps me, but I'm also doing it because I need to change. Just to make myself a bit calmer is not enough. The fact is that God needs to do something fundamental to me. He needs to turn me inside out.'

That is certainly my own experience when I have committed some grave error or when a relationship has gone sour, through my own fault. I had harboured a dislike against an old friend for several years for what my wife and I both felt were good reasons. I sensed that he, too, had grown to dislike me and we had not spoken for many years. That dislike had become part of my mind-set. I had the thought that, if I prayed for him, my feeling would change. It took several months, but gradually I began to feel the warmest sympathy for him. The next time we met, at a funeral, every trace of animus had gone from both of us and we had a delightful talk.

Elizabeth Lester told me a story of how she had been led to mend a relationship. 'There was an older woman called Mary who was in charge of the house where I was living before I got married. She behaved very much like an old-fashioned matron and all us younger women were terribly afraid of her, so afraid that we could hardly manage to say 'good morning!'.

'One day in my time of quiet, I had the most surprising thought – 'treat Mary as if she were your mother'. I reacted fiercely 'no, I can't do that, I love my mum'. Then a second thought came: 'Serve her'. So I tried to take care of Mary and, somehow, came to love her.

'In fact, all my friends began to treat her as a mother and, as that happened, Mary started treating us like daughters. She became a much-loved person. You see, she had had no children of her own, and what we did perhaps warmed her heart and gave her something she had missed terribly'.

Rowan Williams says that a belief in that other voice is now not limited to one part of the Anglican Church, it is no longer a party matter. But was it possible, I asked, that that voice – in Christian terms, the Holy Spirit – was at work in other faiths too?

'Let's look at the theology of this', he replied. 'In his Letter to the Romans, Paul paints a picture of something struggling to come to birth on the earth and that something was the arrival of Jesus, who offered a new and living way for us to grow towards God. With the coming of Jesus, something was unlocked for the whole of the universe'.

That meant that wherever in the world there was a real longing for and openness towards God, the Holy Spirit was at work somewhere in it. The Spirit's work in the world could not be limited. It was doing 'Christ-shaped' things in people whether they were Christian or not, whether they knew it or not.

'My experience of the Spirit', said Graham Tomlin, Bishop of Kensington and previously director of St Mellitus, the largest theological training college in the Anglican Church, 'was of a warming of my heart towards Christ. I have never heard the Spirit speaking in an audible voice, but I have no doubt that there are Christians who do.

'There seem to be people who act like lightning conductors, who have the ability to hear the Spirit in a very clear way'.

Was it possible, I asked, for that Spirit to communicate with people who were non-Christians? 'Look at the book of Genesis', Tomlin replied, 'where it speaks of the Spirit brooding over the face of the waters. In fact, throughout the Old Testament, there is a sense of the Spirit being sent to the whole of creation.

'Take Psalm 104 – 'thou sendeth forth thy Spirit and thou reneweth the face of the earth'. That means to me that the work of the Spirit is to renew the whole creation.

'Saint Basil of Caesarea said that what God created by his Word He perfected through his Spirit, so I believe that the Holy Spirit is at work in the whole of creation and not just the Christian Church. The Church of course draws attention to Christ but you can see the presence of Christ incarnate in other faiths too.

'In John's Gospel, Jesus speaks of the Spirit blowing where it will, so the fact that one can find echoes of Christianity in other faiths is entirely to be expected'.

I am delighted that the lofty dismissiveness towards other faiths which ruled for so long in the Christian Church is beginning to disappear. The marvellous mixture of conviction and openness which Tomlin expresses makes me very happy to be part of my funny old, confused, warring Anglican Church.

Twelve

Questions – and Answers

Writing this book has been, for me, a richly rewarding experience. I had been allowed into the most private places in people's lives, heard the stories of men and women who have risked everything in obeying what they felt was that other voice and marvelled at the results of their obedience.

I had also been pleasantly surprised at how wide a resonance the notion of that other voice seemed to have. Hindus, Muslims and even some Buddhists as well as Christians found in it an echo of their own beliefs.

So many of the people I talked with gave a, to me, thoroughly convincing account of how they believe God has intervened in their lives; and, because of those experiences, firmly believe that the God who has 'spoken' to them, has transformed their lives for the better – and is, furthermore, totally trustworthy and reliable.

Yet their experience – and mine, for that matter – is in no way sufficient to give a definitive answer to the question of whether such a God actually exists, still less whether He (?) is capable of communicating directly with us.

That remains, and will forever remain, the ultimate unfathomable mystery. And since there is, and cannot be any guarantee that a god of any kind exists, it is little more than child's play for a good and scrupulous philosopher to be able to rubbish the notion of God altogether.

'People say that God is intelligent, wise, benevolent, powerful', writes John Hospers, Director of the School of Philosophy at the University of Southern California in Los Angeles, 'that he commands, hears our prayers, desires our welfare, forgives us our trespasses, and so on'. Hospers makes even the 'so on' sound rather contemptuous and dismissive.

'But how', he goes on, 'can the properties people attribute to God literally apply? It is difficult, if not impossible, to imagine all this occurring without any kind of organism – and almost no one today would wish to say that God is a physical organism having eyes, nose, hands, feet and so on' (another 'and so on'!).

'All kinds of personal characteristics are attributed to God, yet how can any being have these characteristics but not have a body of any kind?' And, he adds, how could such a being be spoken of as male or female, since it doesn't have such a body.

It all sounds so simple and indeed obvious; and it makes people such as Niketu Iralu and the Dean of Christ Church sound like deluded fools for harbouring such convictions.

Even those who fervently believe in God find it extremely hard to explain why their supposedly benevolent God chooses to 'intervene' in some cases of profound human need but not in others. On the face of things, such interventions do seem to be, to put it mildly, totally haphazard. Even St Augustine did not succeed in fathoming how God's order in the world actually worked. That, too, is a total mystery.

It is a mystery in which, for once, the glories of the human mind avail us nothing. In one sense, it makes the efforts of both theologians and atheists, believers and unbelievers alike, seem like a complete waste of time. All their wise words and trenchant analyses get us nowhere in the end, because neither camp can come to any watertight conclusion. Could it be, I wonder, that God — if there is a God — has arranged it thus?

For myself, I am glad that it is so, and I say that not to justify the part which I believe God has played in my own life but because I think it would be appalling to conclude that human wisdom is all that we humans and our world have. For all the benefits of scientific advance, has human wisdom delivered the kind of world with which we are happy?

The evidence is very much to the contrary. Human wisdom alone has not, thus far, succeeded in answering our existential and emotional needs, which seem to multiply as faith declines. The more honest among us know how thoroughly inadequate and needy we are of ourselves. That is why I thank heaven that the God question cannot be answered by human ingenuity and cleverness.

A great many people have no interest whatsoever in addressing that question. All too often, they have been completely turned off by what is laughably called 'organised' religion, and have no wish to get involved in the entanglements and uncertainties of the whole God business. Who can blame them?

Yet a good many such people long for something to mitigate the stress of their lives, something which would help them come to terms with all the pressures, something which might also address their admitted spiritual needs.

For them, the practice of mindfulness has seemed positively heaven-sent. It is doctrine-lite, risk-free and requires them to do little more then sit in meditative silence for twenty minutes twice a day. It is, of course, an essentially Buddhist notion, and none the worse for that.

Its proponents claim that the practice will yield all kinds of benefits. Practitioners learn – perforce – how to be still and quiet. That, in turn, can help them to discover a different way of approaching their lives which after all don't, they find, have to be all about doing and problem-solving. There is a kind of life, in other words, which is not all about catching the right train and sending the right email.

Hopefully, as they give themselves to the discipline of daily meditation, they will also feel able to let go of eternally striving to get somewhere or be something – to free themselves from their driven-ness, and in the process, begin to lead infinitely more balanced and happy lives.

It is, in many ways, a very attractive prospectus and has been a boon to many thousands of worn-out, stress-ridden people who have leapt upon it as if it were a raft on a turbulent ocean. Nor do some of its proponents rule out the possibility that, as people practise mindful meditation, they might even become more sensitive to the divine, the 'beyond' should such a thing exist in some form of other.

Others, perhaps touched by the stories in this book may have an instinct to go further, to try to discover whether the idea of that other voice may be enough of a reality to be worth exploring further. If my own experience is anything to go by, they may find the process a good deal simpler and less complicated than they have been led to expect.

There are, of course, an infinite number of ways in which to try to get in touch with that other voice – sitting quietly in some beautiful spot, spending time in retreats of one kind or another. One of the simplest, which evidently helped the people whose stories are told in this book was to give their consciences, and perhaps that other voice, a powerful nudge by allowing the light of absolute moral standards – honesty, purity, unselfishness and love – to play upon the reality of their lives in a time of silence. Those are standards, incidentally, which find a ready resonance in all the major religions.

In the lives of the people whose stories are told here, the results were both varied and productive. Ramez Salame, the Lebanese lawyer, at that time by his own account a total egocentric, was told that he should consider his sisters more and show it by taking them to the cinema. John Lester was told to apologise to his sister for cheating when he played her at tennis. Omnia Mazouk, the ambassador's daughter, was told to stop stealing her father's money from his desk.

Some extraordinarily devious (and rather laughable) behaviour was brought to light. Niketu Iralu, the Naga, was asked to confess to his doctor father that he had been spending his parent's hard-earned cash not on works of the finest English literature but on (no doubt useful) sex manuals. Parthiban was shocked to be asked to return two hundred books to the college library.

Now all those things can be put down to nothing more than their consciences, but can we be quite sure that there is no connection between the voice of conscience and that other voice? Might it just be within the bounds of possibility that the two are always in cahoots? On the other hand, it wasn't conscience which told Amit Mukherjee to 'use a larger needle': it wasn't conscience which told John Lester that he would one day marry Elizabeth McAll: and it was not conscience which told me 'I want you to be a journalist!'

Whichever it was, the thoughts may have been simple but the consequences were always considerable. A veil had been raised and a sharp light shone upon lives which had previously hoped to push shameful behaviour under the carpet. A different will had entered the picture. A new way of living – on different principles – was being proposed. The question now was simple: would the people who had had these uncomfortable thoughts actually obey?

The cost of obedience, after all, seemed high. Parthiban was afraid that it would put his entire future at the college at risk. For Lester, Omnia and Niketu, there was the humiliation of admitting to deplorable behaviour. The images of themselves that they had sedulously cultivated would be shattered, their fallibility would be revealed and they would be required to humble themselves.

And, they might have asked, for what? Only, it seems, because they had seen in that silent assessment of their lives according to the highest standards, a glimpse of a new way of living, a new kind of freedom, a challenge which they could not resist. That was more than the power of conscience. That, in my view, was the power of that other voice, an instinct for the divine which is in all of us.

Each of these people sensed instinctively that they had come to a crucial turning-point in their lives. Perhaps they sensed, too, that their obedience might be infinitely precious to God because they would be acknowledging that He did, indeed, exist and that, for once, they were giving his will primacy in their lives.

It hardly needs saying that we are not, here, talking about those dreadful, hectoring, insulting, destructive 'voices' which afflict a minority of people and with which they need urgent help. All too often, those 'voices' are akin to mental illness and make the lives of those who suffer from them well-nigh unbearable. No, we are talking here about a voice which wishes only well for us, even if obedience to it can seem to carry a considerable cost.

And despite all the quite proper speculation about a God who is supposed to be distant and unpredictable, the God who told these people what they needed to do was only too accessible so far as they were concerned! Would others be so simply led to the starting-line if they tried the same experiment? Is God likely to turn anybody away? I hardly think so.

But how are we to be sure when it is God speaking to us and when it is just our own minds? It is a vital question. We are, after all, infinitely flawed creatures capable of the greatest foolishness and error. Perhaps the first question to ask ourselves is whether the thought we have had is in line with absolute moral standards. And then will what you think you are being told to do heal relationships, reduce suffering, give hope? If there is still some doubt it may be worth discussing the issue with trusted friends before acting.

These, though, were only the first steps of obedience for the people in these stories. They had no idea what lay ahead if they were to continue to follow the promptings of that other voice. In terms of adventure, it scarcely let them down, did it? Ramez has spent his life trying to bring peace and reconciliation to the diverse peoples of his beloved Lebanon, Niketu has done the same in Nagaland. Parthiban spent his time as a bank manager in rural India giving loans to poor people to help them get their tiny businesses off the ground.

In every case, they have had to face the entire range of life's burdens and challenges – illness, profound disappointments, shortage of funds, setbacks and anxieties. They received no special favour except for the sense of a loving presence beside them – and their horizons were always blessedly broad.

The same is true of those whose stories are told here but who have travelled in some ways by a rather different path. Rinchen Khando, wife of the Dalai Lama's younger brother, has laid down her life for the past twenty years in obedience to that other voice to make sure Tibetan nuns are properly educated. Sheikh Nuh and his admirable band of Sufis faithfully uphold the great mystical traditions of Islam. The former Chief Rabbi, Jonathan Sacks, that most brilliant of religious minds who always tries to pay heed to that other voice, has poured out a stream of wisdom in a series of splendid books.

For myself, I'm just relieved and thankful that that other voice led me firmly away from the managerial life and towards the world of words. It knew me, a confused and rather indecisive young man far better than I knew myself. That, I suspect, may be true of all of us. We may, after all, be speaking of our Creator.

Epilogue

One man's experience of That Other Voice:

> I said: 'Let me walk in the fields.'
> He said: 'No, walk in the town.'
> I said: 'There are no flowers there.'
> He said: 'No flowers but a crown.'
>
> I said: 'I shall miss the light,
> And friends will miss me, they say.'
> He answered: 'Choose tonight
> If I am to miss you or they.'
>
> I cast one look at the fields,
> Then set my face to the town:
> He said: 'My child, do you yield?
> Will you leave the flowers for the crown?'
>
> Then into His hand went mine;
> And into my heart came He;
> And I walk in a light divine,
> The path I had feared to see.

Obedience by George MacDonald